D0077061

A Guide for Supervisors and Trainers on Implementing
The Creative Curriculum® for Early Childhood, Third Edition

Diane Trister Dodge

Contributing Writers:

Marilyn Goldhammer
Laura J. Colker
Peter Pizzolongo
Ilene Greenstone

TEACHING STRATEGIES INC.

Washington, DC

Published by

Teaching Strategies, Inc.
P.O. Box 42243
Washington, DC 20015

Distributed by

Gryphon House, Inc.
P.O. Box 275
Mt. Rainier, MD 20712

Copyright © 1993 by Teaching Strategies, Inc.

All rights reserved. No part of this book may be reproduced in any form or by any means without the prior written permission of Teaching Strategies, Inc. except that handouts and charts may be reproduced for training purposes.

ISBN 1-879537-07-9

Library of Congress Card Catalog Number: 92-062949

Publication Date: January, 1993

Acknowledgments

A number of people have contributed to the development of *A Guide for Supervisors and Trainers on Implementing the Creative Curriculum for Early Childhood.* First, I would like to acknowledge the contribution of Marilyn Goldhammer who worked closely with me in designing and drafting many of the workshops outlined in Part Two. As an experienced trainer, Marilyn shared many of her own training strategies in documenting the workshops on the *Creative Curriculum.* I have also benefited in many ways from my work with Peter Pizzolongo and Ruth Uhlmann, who conducted training sessions on the *Creative Curriculum* for Head Start programs during a field test in 1986-87 and greatly enriched the content of the workshops described in Part Two.

The previous edition of this *Guide* was completed while I was at Creative Associates International, Inc., a management consulting firm in Washington, DC during the time I worked with Head Start education coordinators on implementing the *Creative Curriculum.* I am indebted to Clennie H. Murphy, Jr., Deputy Associate Commissioner, and E. Dollie Wolverton, Chief, Education Services Branch, Head Start Bureau, Administration for Children, Youth, and Families, for enabling me to share this training with Head Start programs across the country.

We prepared this new edition of *A Guide for Supervisors and Trainers* in order to address the changes made in the third edition of the *Creative Curriculum.* I want to thank the following colleagues for their contributions: Laura Colker for the workshops on Cooking and Computers, Peter Pizzolongo for preparing the workshops on Music and Movement, Bonnie Kittredge and Ilene Greenstone for helping me to modify the section on Working with Staff. I also want to acknowledge Debra Foulks and Frank Harvey for their support on production, Martha Cooley for editorial assistance, and Beth Hudgins for design and layout.

This *Guide* represents a collection of ideas and strategies acquired and developed during more than 20 years of working with teachers and supervisors. I have undoubtedly adapted and expanded upon the original ideas of other trainers and educators. They have enriched my own repertoire, and if I have failed to acknowledge their contributions, it is only because I can no longer recall where and when I first encountered their excellent ideas. Each time I conduct a workshop on the *Creative Curriculum,* I learn from the participants who generously share their own ideas and experiences. I hope that users of this *Guide* will be enriched in their work as I have been enriched by the work of others throughout my professional life.

Diane Trister Dodge
December 1992

Table of Contents

Page

Introduction

Part One: Supporting Staff on Implementing the *Creative Curriculum*

I.   Introducing the Curriculum 3

II.   Working with Staff 18

III.   Classroom Visits 28

Part Two: Workshops on the *Creative Curriculum*

I.   Workshop Strategies 55

II.   Setting the Stage Workshops 58

III.   Block Workshops 84

IV.   House Corner Workshops 97

V.   Table Toy Workshops 113

VI.   Art Workshops 125

VII.   Sand and Water Workshops 137

VIII.   Library Workshops 145

IX.   Music and Movement Workshops 155

X.   Cooking Workshops 172

XI.   Computer Workshops 185

XII.   Outdoor Workshops 196

Appendices 211

    A. *Creative Curriculum* Self-Assessment and Observation Form 213

    B. Staff Development Forms 235

Introduction

Quality of teaching depends to a substantial extent on the quality of the supervision and training teachers receive. This *Guide* is addressed to early childhood educators who are responsible for staff development. You play a central role in supporting teachers and ensuring that the educational program meets the standards of our profession for quality.

One of your major tasks is to select the curriculum and to support teachers in its implementation. This task is of great importance because the curriculum influences the level of teacher satisfaction and competence, hence the quality of the program itself. In selecting a curriculum, you have probably considered questions such as the following:

- Is it developmentally appropriate?

- Will teachers be able to implement it?

- Is it one that can remain in effect in the face of staff turnover?

- Can it be implemented in a traditional early childhood setting with standard early childhood equipment and materials?

- Does it include a meaningful role for parents?

- Does it include a training program to support my role in supervising and training staff on its implementation?

Each of these questions is answered affirmatively by the *Creative Curriculum*. The *Curriculum* is based on child development theory and is developmentally appropriate for preschool and kindergarten children. Teachers with little experience, as well as seasoned teachers, have been able to understand its philosophy and approach and have learned how to implement it in their communities. Program consistency is enhanced by the *Creative Curriculum* because even with staff turnover, new teachers can quickly appreciate the environmental focus and learn the value of each interest area. Programs adopting the *Curriculum* do not have to purchase special equipment or materials—the *Curriculum* uses the traditional preschool environment as its structure. It recognizes parents as the primary educators in children's lives and emphasizes a strong parent-teacher partnership in all aspects of the program. And finally, the *Creative Curriculum* offers a comprehensive training program, including audiovisual materials to support its implementation.

The purpose of this *Guide* is to support your role as a supervisor and trainer in helping teachers implement the *Creative Curriculum*. There are many ways to work with staff to ensure that the program they provide meets the standards of the profession for quality and developmental appropriateness. As a supervisor, you define program standards, clarify expectations, and support staff in meeting their goals. You establish a climate that nurtures growth and learning, provide staff with the materials they need, and spend time observing and providing feedback on what is happening in their classrooms. Classroom visits are the best way to determine if the curriculum is being implemented effectively and appropriately. To make these visits most useful, you must have a clear idea of what to look for and how to guide teachers when their practices are inappropriate. Part One of this *Guide* addresses these aspects of supervision.

Part Two outlines specific workshops for conveying the *Creative Curriculum* to staff. Many of these workshops are equally appropriate for parents, volunteers, and others involved in the program. The workshops are designed for hands-on learning. Time periods for each set of workshops are not included because each trainer will select and adapt the workshop strategies to suit her or his own training style, the needs of participants, and the time allotted for training.

Two audiovisual resources are recommended for use in training. *The New Room Arrangement as a Teaching Strategy*, a slide presentation in VHS format, provides concrete ideas on how different classroom arrangements affect children's behavior. The videotape on the *Creative Curriculum* shows how children learn in each interest area and the teacher's role in facilitating learning through play. Information on where to obtain each of these resources can be found on the back page of this *Guide*.

Part One

Supporting Staff on Implementing the *Creative Curriculum*

                                                                      Page

I.   **Introducing the Curriculum**... 3

     When Should Supervisors Consider a New Curriculum? 3

     Advantages of an Environmentally Based Curriculum............................. 6

     Standards of the Profession.. 8

II. **Working with Staff**.. 18

     Self-Motivation: The Key to Enhancing Staff Competence........................ 18

     Creating a Positive Climate for Learning 19

     Planning Staff Development... 21

     Observing and Recording Teacher Behaviors.................................... 24

     The Feedback Conference.. 25

III. **Classroom Visits** 28

     The Environment 28

     Equipment and Materials.. 31

     Program Structure: Schedule and Routines..................................... 38

     Activities and Experiences... 41

     Supportive Interactions and Positive Social Development....................... 44

     Individualizing 47

     Parent Involvement... 49

I. Introducing the Curriculum

In introducing a new curriculum to your staff, it is helpful if you can explain how you selected it and why you feel it is appropriate for your program. Providing a clear rationale can make the difference in whether or not the curriculum is accepted by staff, administrators, and parents. This chapter discusses some of the reasons a supervisor may have for selecting a developmentally appropriate curriculum and the advantages of an environmental approach. It discusses the standards in our profession for a quality program and shows how the *Creative Curriculum* addresses guidelines for a developmentally appropriate program developed by the National Association for the Education of Young Children (NAEYC). In this chapter, you will also find suggestions for creating a positive climate for learning and setting up a system for assisting each staff member's development.

When Should Supervisors Consider a New Curriculum?

One common reason for selecting a new curriculum is to address problems in the program. There are several warning signs that may alert you to the possibility that your program is "off track." Listed below are eight warning signs, some examples that illustrate the problems, and possible causes. When you can identify the reasons behind a problem, you can more effectively plan your goals for staff development.

WARNING SIGN #1: *Children are not purposefully involved*

Examples	Possible Causes
• Children wander around the room aimlessly during choice time.	• Activity choices are not obvious.
• Children have trouble selecting an activity.	• Toys and materials are poorly organized and not attractively displayed.
• Involvement in any one area or activity is shortlived.	• Activity areas are too open so children are distracted easily.
• Play is simple and repetitive.	• Materials are not complex enough to hold children's interest and challenge their thinking skills.
	• Children lack the skills to engage in a high level of socio-dramatic play.

WARNING SIGN #2: *Children show little respect for materials*

Examples	Possible Causes
• Puzzle pieces are used for food in the house corner. • Community helpers from the block corner may be found in the water table or the art shelf. • Books in the library have crayon marks and torn pages. • Clean-up is a free-for-all: children place materials carelessly on the shelves.	• Places for each object or set of materials are not defined and clearly labeled. • Lack of organization in the arrangement of materials conveys that order is not respected. • Teachers have not introduced materials to children and explained the rules for their use.

WARNING SIGN #3: *Children fight over materials*

Examples	Possible Causes
• Some children tend to monopolize favorite materials. • Teachers are continually arbitrating disputes.	• The demands on children to share are not age-appropriate. • More duplicates of toys and materials are needed. • There are too few choices offered. • Teachers have not helped children learn how to negotiate for turns.

WARNING SIGN #4: *Children are often in large groups*

Examples	Possible Causes
• Circle times last 20-30 minutes and children have trouble staying still. • A large portion of each day is spent on custodial tasks such as preparing for meals, cleaning up, brushing teeth, toileting, and transitions. • Everyone goes through routines at the same time, so waiting periods are unnecessarily long.	• Teachers feel more in control when the whole group is involved in the same activity. • They want to be sure everyone learns the same concepts and skills. • Teachers feel that they do most of their teaching at circle time. • The classroom is not organized into separate activity areas.

WARNING SIGN #5: *Children are not purposefully involved in activities outdoors*

Examples	Possible Causes
• Running is the main activity. • Few activities are offered to involve children in more focused play. • Outdoor time is limited to 10-15 minutes. • Teachers use the outdoor time to chat with one another and socialize, rather than to interact with the children.	• Teachers do not view the outdoors as a rich learning environment for children. • They have not created distinct areas or offered a selection of activities. • Teachers are not adequately dressed for cold weather. • This period of the day is viewed as a break for children and for teachers.

WARNING SIGN #6: *Teachers are continually testing children*

Examples	Possible Causes
• The questions teachers ask children are designed to test them: "What color is this?" or "How many do you have?" • Teachers use work sheets and dittos as a way of teaching skills and concepts. • Standardized tests are used to assess what children know.	• Teachers feel they are accountable for what children learn and believe they are teaching children concepts when they ask testing questions. • Teachers are not skilled in asking open-ended questions. • Teachers want children to succeed in school and feel this is the best way to achieve this goal.

WARNING SIGN #7: *Teachers have lost their spontaneity and joyfulness*

Examples	Possible Causes
• Teachers follow the same lesson plans they developed years ago. • Children's interests and questions are not used to plan experiences and extend learning. • Teachers have a low energy level and rarely laugh with the children. • The day seems to be one routine after another.	• The program is using a prescriptive curriculum. • Teachers feel compelled to "cover" certain content areas with the children and therefore resist being "side-tracked" by a spontaneous event or interest. • Teachers are not encouraged to be creative and to try out new ideas.

WARNING SIGN #8: *Teachers are feeling defensive about allowing children to play*

Examples	Possible Causes
• A central focus of the program is getting children ready for elementary school. • Teachers talk about pressures from parents to teach the children and prepare them for reading and math. • Teachers know that children learn through play but they limit the play time to allow more time for group instruction and teacher-directed activities.	• Teachers are unable to articulate their philosophy and beliefs about early childhood education and therefore feel unprepared to respond to pressures from parents and the community for an academic program. • It is easier to see what children are learning when they are taught by drill and repetition.

Many of these warning signs can be addressed by the selection and implementation of a developmentally appropriate curriculum that focuses on the learning environment.

Advantages of an Environmentally Based Curriculum

A carefully organized and rich environment can serve as the focus for an early childhood curriculum. An environmental focus has multiple benefits for both staff and program development. Once teachers organize their space and materials in the recommended ways, they see immediate and positive results. As they observe children at play and practice appropriate interactions, they develop a practical understanding of the curriculum's philosophy and approach. Teachers and parents need to appreciate how children learn through interactions with other children, adults, and the environment.

An environmentally based curriculum is a vehicle for achieving a developmentally appropriate program. This is true for a number of reasons.

- **It is a concrete and practical approach to defining a curriculum.** Teachers can readily understand the approach and implement the suggestions. Once established, the curriculum can be maintained in spite of staff turnover. Parents can see concrete evidence that the environment is structured to support learning.

- **It keeps the focus for planning on the environment.** The environment is the "textbook" for the curriculum. An environmentally based curriculum requires teachers to continually assess children's use of the environment and make decisions on how to enrich each interest area, to address children's emerging interests and needs.

- **It conforms with what we know about how young children learn.** One of the most important goals in early childhood education is to develop in children the desire to learn and continue learning. Because learning is an active and social process, it is maximized when children are actively engaged in interactions with materials, peers, and adults.

- **It supports children's social development.** Children develop social skills when they have many opportunities to interact with peers and adults one-to-one and in small groups. One important goal of early childhood education is to help each child to be able to establish and maintain friendships. The environment can be structured to support small group interactions and to encourage sharing and cooperative ventures.

- **It offers one of the best strategies for individualizing the program.** A well-planned environment frees teachers to observe how children use materials and work with peers. An environmentally based curriculum gives teachers more time to interact with children to guide and extend their learning. When offered a variety of choices, children tend to select and stay with activities that are developmentally appropriate for them.

- **It reduces the stress teachers experience in more structured and academic programs.** A curriculum founded on a well-organized environment supports teachers as well as children. Because children are better able to select their own activities, stay meaningfully involved, and return materials when they are finished, teachers have more time to interact positively with children. Teachers spend less time on maintenance tasks and discipline.

- **It offers a clear framework for planning and implementing a developmentally appropriate program.** An environmentally based curriculum sets forth the program's philosophy, specific goals and objectives for children, how to set up the environment, a well-defined role for teachers as facilitators of learning, and a meaningful role for parents that complements and extends the curriculum. It gives teachers the freedom to be creative in their teaching rather than requiring them to adhere to a specific sequence of activities or learning goals. It encourages teachers to be flexible and spontaneous in responding to children's actions and interactions.

- **Its philosophy, approach, and outcomes can be clearly explained and demonstrated to parents.** The approach can be related to parents' real-life experiences—what learning experiences have been most meaningful to them. It lends itself to hands-on activities to help parents understand what and how their children are learning when they interact with real objects, materials, and people in the environment.

The *Creative Curriculum* is a comprehensive curriculum that provides the framework for any developmentally appropriate program for preschool and kindergarten children. The framework of the curriculum includes:

- **A statement of philosophy**—the beliefs and theories that guide curriculum development and implementation, including an understanding of how children develop physically, socio-emotionally, and intellectually.

- **Goals and objectives**—the skills, attitudes, and understandings targeted for mastery.

- **The physical environment**—specific guidance on the importance of room arrangement and how to select and display materials to support the development of trust, independence, and initiative.

- **The teacher's role**—a clear definition of teaching strategies that promote learning and growth.

- **The parent's role**—a commitment to the joint partnership of parents and teachers in promoting each child's growth and development.

Standards of the Profession

Another reason for selecting and implementing a developmentally appropriate curriculum is to ensure that your program meets the profession's standards for quality. Substantial agreement exists in the field of early childhood education on what constitutes high-quality care and education for young children. Experts agree that a high-quality early childhood program must be developmentally appropriate. This means that:

- children learn at their own pace through active involvement with materials, with peers and adults;

- the environment is well planned and includes a rich variety of materials and choices;

- teachers ask questions that expand children's play and support a positive self-concept; and

- parents play a meaningful role in the program and have a good understanding of its philosophy and goals.

Several standards of quality have been established by the early childhood profession. These standards, which specify the criteria for developmental appropriateness, include the following:

- *Developmentally Appropriate Practice in Early Childhood Programs Serving Children from Birth Through Age 8*, National Association for the Education of Young Children (NAEYC), Washington, DC, 1987.

- *Head Start Program Performance Standards*, Head Start Bureau, Administration for Children, Youth, and Families, Office of Human Development Services, U.S. Department of Health and Human Services, Washington, DC, 1975.

- *Accreditation Criteria and Procedures of the National Academy of Early Childhood Programs*, NAEYC, Washington, DC, 1984.

In recent years, a number of organizations have published standards for public school programs serving children from four to eight years of age.

- *Right from the Start, The Report of the NASBE Task Force on Early Childhood Education*, National Association of State Boards of Education, Alexandria, VA, 1988.

- *Standards for Quality Programs for Young Children: Early Childhood Education and the Elementary School Principal*, National Association of Elementary School Principals, Alexandria, VA, 1990.

- *Early Childhood Education and the Public Schools*, National Education Association (NEA) Standing Committee on Instruction and Professional Development, 1990.

- *Kindergarten Policies: What is Best for Children?* Joanna T. Peck, Ginny McCaig, and Mary Ellen Sapp, NAEYC, Washington, DC, 1988.

Standards for staff competence in implementing a high-quality, developmentally appropriate curriculum are set forth by the Council for Early Childhood Professional Recognition. The criteria described in the *Child Development Associate (CDA) Competency Standards* serve as a way of measuring the performance of caregivers and teachers in 13 functional areas: safe, healthy, learning environment, physical, cognitive, communication, creative, self, social, guidance, families, program management, and professionalism.

The charts that follow illustrate how the *Creative Curriculum* addresses NAEYC's standards for developmentally appropriate practice in programs serving three-year-olds and four- and five-year-olds.

HOW THE *CREATIVE CURRICULUM* SUPPORTS DEVELOPMENTALLY APPROPRIATE PRACTICE IN PROGRAMS SERVING THREE-YEAR-OLDS

While many of the program practices recommended for fours and fives are also appropriate for threes, there are some special considerations that should not be overlooked in providing a developmentally appropriate program for this age group. Using the guidelines suggested by the National Association for the Education of Young Children (NAEYC) for programs serving three-year-old children, the chart below illustrates how *The Creative Curriculum for Early Childhood* addresses the developmental needs of this age group.

Appropriate Practice[*]	*The Creative Curriculum*
• Adults provide affection and support, comforting children when they cry and reassuring them when fearful. Adults plan experiences to alleviate children's fears.	• Explains children's socio-emotional growth and how teachers can promote trust. Shows how dramatic play helps children deal with fears and recommends books and activities that alleviate these fears.
• Adults support 3-year-olds' play and developing independence, helping when needed, but allowing them to do what they are capable of doing and what they want to do for themselves ("I can do it myself!").	• Shows how to create an environment that supports children's independence. Defines the teacher's role in supporting play in all interest areas.
• Adults recognize that, although 3-year-olds are usually more cooperative than toddlers and want to please adults, they may revert to toddler behavior (thumb-sucking, crying, hitting, baby talk) when they are feeling shy or upset, especially in a new situation. Adults know that 3-year-olds' interest in babies, and especially their own recent infancy, provides an opportunity for children to learn about themselves and human development.	• Provides practical ideas for creating a soft and comfortable environment. Emphasizes a homelike environment in the house corner to support role playing of family experiences. Suggests books on babies and family themes.
• Adults provide opportunities for 3-year-olds to demonstrate and practice their newly developed self-help skills and their desire to help adults with dressing and undressing, toileting, feeding themselves (including helping with pouring milk or setting the table), brushing teeth, washing hands, and helping pick up toys. Adults are patient with occasional toileting accidents, spilled food, and unfinished jobs.	• Shows how to create an environment that supports independence by organizing materials logically on low shelves and labeling the place for each object; this makes clean up an enjoyable game and a learning activity. Provides guidance on establishing routines and allowing ample time for children to participate at their own pace. Recognizes that routines such as meal times, dressing, teeth brushing, naptime, and clean up are valuable learning times.

[*]   Sue Bredekamp (ed). *Developmentally Appropriate Practice in Programs Serving Children Birth Through Age 8* (Washington, DC: NAEYC, 1987), pp. 47–50.

Appropriate Practice	The Creative Curriculum
• Adults know that growth rates may slow down and appetites decrease at this age. Children are encouraged to eat "tastes" in small portions with the possibility of more servings if desired.	• Gives practical suggestions for making meal times enjoyable times for children.
• Adults guide 3-year-olds to take naps or do restful activities periodically throughout the day, recognizing that these younger children may exhaust themselves—especially when trying to keep up with older children in the group.	• Offers strategies for helping children ease into naptime and for helping children who are unable to sleep. Suggests organizing the environment to create private and soft spaces where children can get away from the group and be alone when they need quiet times.
• Adults provide many opportunities for 3s to play by themselves, next to another child (parallel play), or with one or two other children. Adults recognize that 3-year-olds are not comfortable with much group participation. Adults read a story or play music with small groups and allow children to enter and leave the group at will.	• Organizes the environment into ten distinct interest areas where children can play alone or near one or two other children. Describes parallel play as a normal stage of development and advocates self-initiated activities in which children make their own choices. Promotes reading to small groups.
• Adults support children's beginning friendships, recognizing that such relationships ("my best friend") are short-lived and may consist of acting silly together or chasing for a few minutes. When conflicts arise, the 3-year-old will often return to playing alone. Adults encourage children to take turns and share but do not always expect children to give up favored items.	• Recognizes the importance of social development and shows teachers how to help children work cooperatively and resolve conflicts. Suggests ways of organizing the environment to minimize the demands on children to share and offers strategies for making sharing and waiting easier for children.
• Adults provide plenty of space and time indoors and outdoors for children to explore and exercise their large muscle skills like running, jumping, galloping, riding a tricycle, or catching a ball, with adults close by to offer assistance as needed.	• Emphasizes the value of outdoor time and suggests ways of organizing space to give children a range of choices during outdoor play.
• Adults provide large amounts of uninterrupted time for children to persist at self-chosen tasks and activities and to practice and perfect their newly developed physical skills if they choose.	• Outlines a daily schedule that allows ample time for children to select their own activities both indoors and outside. Recommends that teachers be flexible in following the schedule when children are involved in activities.

Appropriate Practice	*The Creative Curriculum*
• Adults provide many materials and opportunities for children to develop fine motor skills such as puzzles, pegboards, beads to string, construction sets, and art materials (crayons, brushes, paints, markers, play dough, blunt scissors). Although children's scribbles are more controlled than those of toddlers, and 3-year-olds will create designs with horizontal and vertical strokes, and will sometimes name their drawings and paintings, adults do not expect a representational product. Art is viewed as creative expression and exploration of materials.	• Explains how to select materials and organize attractive and appropriate areas for art and table toy activities. Illustrates stages of development in using toys and in drawing and painting. Emphasizes art experiences as a creative and open-ended process rather than for the purpose of producing products.
• Adults provide plenty of materials and time for children to explore and learn about the environment, to exercise their natural curiosity, and to experiment with cause and effect relationships. For example, they provide blocks (that children line up first and later may build into towers); more complex dramatic play props (for playing work and family roles and animals); sand and water with tools for pouring, measuring, and scooping; many toys and tools to experiment with like knobs, latches, and any toy that opens, closes, and can be taken apart; and simple science activities like blowing bubbles, flying kites, or planting seeds.	• Views the environment as the central focus for curriculum planning and shows how to organize activities around seven interest areas: blocks, house corner, table toys, art, sand and water, library, and outdoors. Suggests appropriate equipment and materials for each area that are developmentally appropriate and engage children in active learning. Explains how children learn in each area and develop and practice new skills.
• Adults encourage children's developing language by speaking clearly and frequently to individual children and listening to their responses. Adults respond quickly and appropriately to children's verbal initiatives. They recognize that talking may be more important than listening for 3-year-olds. Adults patiently answer children's questions ("Why?" "How come?") and recognize that 3-year-olds often ask questions they know the answers to in order to open a discussion or practice giving answers themselves. Adults know that children are rapidly acquiring language, experimenting with verbal sounds, and beginning to use language to solve problems and learn concepts.	• Describes typical questions children ask and why. Emphasizes the importance of talking with children and gives specific examples of comments and questions teaching can pose as children play in each interest area. Explains how children develop oral communication skills and the teacher's role in promoting language skills including specific strategies and activities.

Appropriate Practice	*The Creative Curriculum*
• Adults provide many experiences and opportunities to extend children's language and musical abilities. Adults read books to one child or a small group; recite simple poems, nursery rhymes, and finger plays; encourage children to sing songs and listen to recordings; facilitate children's play of circle and movement games like London Bridge, Farmer in the Dell, and Ring Around the Rosie; provide simple rhythm instruments; listen to stories that children tell or write down stories they dictate; and enjoy 3-year-olds' sense of humor.	• Shows how to create an attractive and well stocked library corner for looking at books and listening to stories and tapes. Offers practical suggestions for reading stories that actively involve children, and for engaging children in story telling and in developing their own original books.
• Adults know that 3-year-olds do not usually understand or remember the rules. Guidance reasons that are specific to a real situation and that are demonstrated repeatedly are more likely to impress young children.	• Offers strategies for organizing an environment that promotes positive behavior: manipulating the environment rather than the children. Shows how appropriate activities and materials and a well balanced schedule engage children in positive interactions.
• Adults provide a safe, hazard-free environment and careful supervision. Adults recognize that 3-year-olds often overestimate their newly developed physical powers and will try activities that are unsafe or beyond their ability (especially in multiage groups where they may model 4- and 5-year-olds). Adults protect children's safety in these situations while also helping them deal with their frustration and maintain their self-confidence ("Joel can tie his shoe because he's 5; when you're 5, you'll probably know how to tie, too.").	• Presents concrete ideas for organizing a safe environment. Emphasizes the role of adults in supervision and ensuring children's safety at all times.

HOW THE *CREATIVE CURRICULUM* SUPPORTS DEVELOPMENTALLY APPROPRIATE PRACTICE IN PROGRAMS SERVING FOUR- AND FIVE-YEAR OLDS

Component	Appropriate Practice*	*Creative Curriculum*
Curriculum goals	Experiences are provided that meet children's needs and stimulate learning in all developmental areas—physical, social, emotional, and intellectual.	Uses an environmentally based approach and describes how teachers can use all interest areas to promote children's growth in cognitive, socio-emotional, and physical development.
	Each child is viewed as a unique person with an individual pattern and timing of growth and development. The curriculum and adult's interaction are responsive to individual differences in ability and interests. Different levels of ability, development, and learning styles are expected, accepted, and used to design appropriate activities.	Describes developmental stages in each interest area, stressing individual differences and how to address them. Focuses on child-initiated activities, how to observe each child's actions to assess his or her level of development, and how to expand the environment based on children's progress and interest.
	Interactions and activities are designed to develop children's self-esteem and positive feelings toward learning.	Fosters independent learning in an appealing and well-organized environment; stresses the provision of successful experiences for children; outlines teaching strategies that avoid the use of judgmental statements; and suggests developmentally appropriate ways for children to learn to take turns and share.
Teaching strategies	Teachers prepare the environment for children to learn through active exploration and interactions with adults, other children, and materials.	Organizes the curriculum around ten interest areas: blocks, house corner, music and movement, table toys, art, sand and water, library, cooking, computers, and outdoors. Promotes appropriate use of materials and shows how children learn new concepts and skills from their daily interactions in the room.
	Children select many of their own activities from among a variety of learning areas the teacher prepares, including dramatic play, blocks, science, math games and puzzles, books, recordings, art, and music.	Stresses the display of materials on labeled shelves and pegboards so that children are able to select activities by themselves. Organizes the environment into seven interest areas.
	Children are expected to be physically and mentally active. Children choose from among activities the teacher has set up or the children spontaneously initiate.	Emphasizes child-initiated activities and encourages the use of concrete materials for children's play. Gives specific words for adults to use to encourage and extend children's active play.

* Sue Bredekamp (ed). *Developmentally Appropriate Practice in Programs Serving Children Birth Through Age 8* (Washington, DC: NAEYC, 1987), pp. 54–57.

Component	Appropriate Practice	*Creative Curriculum*
Teaching strategies (continued)	Children work individually or in small, informal groups most of the time.	Organizes the room into distinct work areas. Focuses on individual and small group play in the blocks, house corner, art, table toys, and reading areas, as well as experiences with sand, water, food, woodworking materials, and outdoor play equipment.
	Children are provided concrete learning activities with materials and people relevant to their own life experiences.	Incorporates homemade, collected, and commercial toys and props reflective of the children's cultures. Encourages parental involvement in the daily program.
	Teachers move among groups and individuals to facilitate children's involvement with materials and activities by asking questions, offering suggestions, or adding more complex materials or ideas to a situation.	Provides comments and questions for teachers to use that are nonjudgmental and focus on expanding play and encouraging children to talk.
	Teachers accept that there is often more than one right answer. Teachers recognize that children learn from self-directed problem solving and experimentation.	Provides ways for teachers to talk with children about their work by describing what they see and asking open-ended questions as children explore materials and learn by doing. Illustrates the kinds of problems children can solve in each interest area and how experimentation can be encouraged.
Guidance of socio-emotional development	Teachers facilitate development of self-control in children by using positive guidance techniques such as modeling and encouraging expected behavior, redirecting children to a more acceptable activity, and setting clear limits. Teachers' expectations match and respect children's developing capabilities.	Provides strategies for creating an environment that helps children develop self-control. Gives teachers concrete ideas for guiding children's behavior in positive and supportive ways. Addresses common problems in each interest area and shows how to overcome them.
	Children are provided many opportunities to develop social skills, such as cooperating, helping, negotiating, and talking with the person involved to solve interpersonal problems. Teachers facilitate the development of these positive skills at all times.	Emphasizes small group and self-selected activities in which children have many opportunities to interact with one another. Demonstrates how teachers can promote problem solving and readiness to share.

Component	Appropriate Practice	*Creative Curriculum*
Language development and literacy	Children are provided many opportunities to see how reading and writing are useful before they are instructed in letter names, sounds, and word identification. Basic skills develop when they are meaning-ful to children. An abundance of these types of activities is provided to develop language and literacy through meaning-ful experience: listening to and reading stories and poems; taking field trips; dictating stories; seeing classroom charts and other print in use; participating in dramatic play and other experiences requiring communication; talking informally with other children and adults; and experimenting with writing and drawing, copying, and inventing their own spelling.	Illustrates how a rich and thoughtfully planned library corner can be used to foster a love for books and stories and an interest in writing. Includes time in the schedule to read books each day. Promotes communication skills in each interest area by giving teachers questioning techniques to promote language development and strategies for storytelling, sign writing in the block area, and labeling of each area.
Cognitive development	Children develop understanding of concepts about themselves, others, and the world around them through observa-tion, interacting with people and real objects, and seeking solutions to concrete problems. Learning about math, science, social studies, health, and other content areas is all integrated through meaningful activities such as those which occur as children build with blocks; measure sand, water, or ingredients for cooking; observe changes in the environment; work with wood and tools; sort objects for a purpose; explore animals, plants, water, wheels, and gears; sing and listen to music from various cultures; and draw, paint, and work with clay. Routines are followed that help children keep themselves healthy and safe.	Outlines cognitive goals and objectives that can be addressed in each interest area and shows how children acquire new concepts and understanding through active play with materials. Advocates starting with the here and now and expanding children's experiences gradually. Shows how all areas are related and demonstrates how children acquire skills in all interest areas. Illustrates how to continually change the environment to challenge children and extend learning. Gives teachers questions to ask to encourage thinking and problem solving.
Physical development	Children have daily opportunities to use large muscles, including running, jumping, and balancing. Outdoor activity is planned daily so children can develop large muscle skills, learn about outdoor environments, and express themselves freely and loudly.	Identifies goals and objectives for physical development. Treats the outdoor environment as a rich setting for learning. Shows teachers how to create a varied outdoor environment to provide choices for children. Allocates ample time for outdoor play in the schedule and explains how teachers can extend learning.

Component	Appropriate Practice	*Creative Curriculum*
Physical development (continued)	Children have daily opportunities to develop small muscle skills through play activities such as pegboards, puzzles, painting, cutting, and other similar activities.	Explains how children develop small muscle skills in each interest area. Provides guidance on how to select table toys and art materials appropriate for young children, and the teacher's role in providing opportunities for children to develop small muscle skills through increasingly challenging use of materials.
Aesthetic development	Children have daily opportunities for aesthetic expression and appreciation through art and music. Children experiment and enjoy various forms of music. A variety of art media is available for creative expression, such as easel and finger painting and clay.	Emphasizes the importance of process over product in activities and provides teachers with practical ideas for creating a stimulating and appealing art area. Lists basic and supplemental art materials. Allocates time each day for creative art experiences and music activities.
Motivation	Children's natural curiosity and desire to make sense of their world are used to motivate them to become involved in learning activities.	Explains the philosophy and theory of how children learn to underscore the importance of helping children make sense of the world in their own ways. Shows teachers how to build on children's interests and discoveries to extend learning.
Parent-teacher relations	Teachers work in partnership with parents, communicating regularly to build mutual understanding and greater consistency for children.	Supports a partnership with parents by providing specific strategies for enhancing communication and promoting understanding. Shows how to work with parents to extend learning in each interest area. Suggests workshops and informal strategies for sharing the curriculum with parents; includes sample letters to parents regarding the program.
Assessment of children	Decisions that have a major impact on children (such as enrollment, retention, assignment to remedial classes) are based primarily on information obtained from observations by teachers and parents, not on the basis of a single test score. Developmental assessment of children's progress and achievement is used to plan curriculum, identify children with special needs, communicate with parents, and evaluate the program's effectiveness.	Stresses the importance of ongoing observations and recording of children's behavior, interests, skills, and interactions as a way to assess and individualize the program for each child. Gives specific developmental stages for children in each interest area as a structure for observing and recording children's progress.

II. Working with Staff

As a supervisor responsible for implementing a developmentally appropriate program, your role is critical. The quality of teaching depends on the quality of supervision teachers receive. This chapter presents strategies for working with staff to support their role in implementing a developmentally appropriate program.

Self-Motivation: The Key to Enhancing Staff Competence

As a supervisor you have probably often asked yourself the question, "How can I motivate teachers to do their jobs well?" The answer to that question is probably, "You can't!" Most adults rarely perform better because of things that others do for them. They perform better because they are self-motivated; they seek out learning experiences that help them improve their skills.

Encouraging self-motivation is an important step in helping staff perform their jobs in a more competent way. One strategy for accomplishing this task is to identify what teachers find satisfying about their role and to focus on enhancing these factors, while at the same time attempting to overcome frustrations.

In a survey of 64 teachers in 24 New England child care programs, the following factors were identified as major sources of satisfaction at work:[1]

- observing progress in children;
- relationships with children;
- challenge of the work;
- pride in performing a service;
- relationships with parents; and
- recognition shown by staff.

The survey also uncovered factors that were sources of frustration for teachers. These factors included the following:

- rate of pay;
- prospects for advancement;
- physical work environment;
- style of supervision;
- number of hours worked; and
- inflexible personnel policies.

One approach to increasing staff competence is to try to improve the factors that frustrate teachers. Doing so has been shown to have a positive effect on teachers. However, dealing with the frustrating factors has very little impact on teachers' level of competence. To promote staff competence, it is more effective to focus on enhancing the sources of satisfaction (the "motivators").

---

[1] Based on Roger Neugebauer, "Self-Motivation: Motivation at Its Best," *Child Care Information Exchange* (October 1984), pp. 7-10.

Implementing *The Creative Curriculum for Early Childhood* can help you focus on the factors that provide satisfaction to teachers of young children, in the following ways.

- **Observing progress in children.** The *Creative Curriculum* outlines specific goals and objectives for children in each area of the learning environment. It defines developmental stages in children's use of each area to assist teachers in assessing progress.

- **Relationships with children.** By giving teachers strategies for organizing the environment that support their role and children's learning, the *Creative Curriculum* frees teachers to spend more time involved in positive interactions with children. It clearly explains the teacher's role in promoting learning and growth and how to build positive relationships with each child.

- **Challenge of the work.** Teachers need to feel that they are personally responsible for their work. The *Creative Curriculum* offers a framework for structuring a developmentally appropriate program. Within this framework, teachers have the freedom to design activities and interactions that will enhance children's learning. It is not a prescribed course of study or a set of activities. Rather, the curriculum encourages teachers to be creative and to continually expand the program.

- **Pride in performing a service.** Teachers need feedback and recognition for their accomplishments. This *Guide* outlines specific job behaviors for teachers and strategies for observing and providing feedback to staff. When teachers share the program with parents (as outlined in each module of the *Creative Curriculum*), parents gain a good understanding of a developmentally appropriate program and the important role that teachers play in their child's development.

- **Relationships with parents.** Parent involvement is one of the basic tenets of the *Creative Curriculum*. Strategies for establishing a partnership with parents and for ensuring ongoing communication and understanding are outlined in "Setting the Stage." A section of each module provides specific and practical ideas for sharing the curriculum with parents and involving them in extending learning at home. A booklet, *A Parent's Guide to Early Childhood Education*, explains a developmentally appropriate program to parents.

- **Recognition by staff.** You can build a climate of mutual respect and recognition among the staff by using training approaches that enable staff to share their knowledge and learn from each other. The training strategies and workshops described in this *Guide* can help in this process.

Creating a Positive Climate for Learning

Supervisors are often in the position of asking staff to change their ideas about teaching and learning and to modify their approaches to curriculum. Change is always difficult, especially in teaching, because all of us come to this profession with preconceived ideas about how teachers teach and how children learn. These ideas come from our own experiences in school, and they may be very different from what we now call "developmentally appropriate practice."

Early childhood educators are asked to give a great deal of themselves in their work with young children. Addressing the social, emotional, physical, and cognitive needs of young children is demanding work. The hours are usually long and the compensation is too often inadequate. In many programs, staff members are not treated as professionals; their ideas are not sought, they are not listened to, and they are not treated with dignity.

Supervisors who want to make changes in the curriculum and enhance staff competence in carrying out a developmentally appropriate program begin by creating a positive climate for learning. When staff members feel that their ideas and skills are respected, they are more open to examining new approaches. When they know that they will be supported rather than judged, they are more willing to take risks and to deal with failure as part of the learning process. And when everyone is committed to a vision of quality care and education, positive changes for children, staff, and families will be more likely to happen.

Listed below are some of the ways that supervisors can create a positive climate for learning.

- **Empower the adult learner.** People who experience a sense of power over their own lives have less need to dominate others, including the children they teach. When you give staff members an opportunity to identify their own needs, to set priorities for their own development, to plan when and how they will participate in staff development sessions, they will be more committed to achieving the goals they set.

- **Build a shared vision for the program.** Take time to develop a vision statement for your program. Involve staff in discussing their own experiences in school and how they learn best. Talk about what it was like for them growing up and how it is different for children today. Share the research and the standards of the early childhood profession as discussed in the previous section. Decide on a message that your program wants to convey to all children and families who are served. When everyone in the program shares a common vision, it is easier to agree on how to achieve that vision.

- **Individualize staff development.** There are many different ways to learn about a topic or acquire specific skills—reading, watching a film or video, observing colleagues, participating in a workshop, peer coaching, classroom support, discussions, and so on. Try to learn about and accommodate each teacher's preferred learning style. The concerns and interests of a teacher just entering the early childhood profession will vary greatly from those of an experienced teacher. Yet all teachers have life experiences and self-knowledge that can be used to help them assess their training needs and plan appropriate staff development.

- **Convey respect for each person.** Most adults you supervise take considerable pride in their work. Although they may not always work with children in ways that you want, it is important to respect their efforts. Give recognition for the positive skills you observe teachers using. Try to build on the satisfaction they have in helping children develop to encourage their own continued development in the field.

- **Provide opportunities for professional dialogues about teaching and learning.** Teachers learn a great deal from one another and value the opportunity to talk about what is happening in their classrooms. One of the best ways to encourage teachers to be reflective about their teaching practices and what is happening to the children in their classrooms is to provide time for them to share with one another. Sharing snacks or a meal together makes it a social event and establishes a relaxed environment.

- **Involve staff in active learning experiences.** An important principle of adult learning, which has been supported by extensive research, is that people learn best when they are actively involved in the learning process. The illustration that follows shows various ways in which people learn and how much they remember from each learning mode. When you are designing training, it is important to include many opportunities for active learning.

How People Learn*

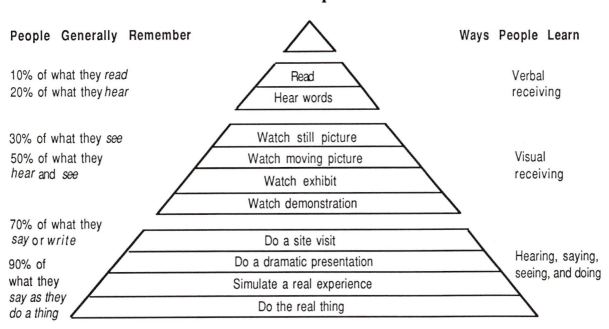

People Generally Remember		Ways People Learn
10% of what they *read*	Read	Verbal receiving
20% of what they *hear*	Hear words	
30% of what they *see*	Watch still picture	Visual receiving
50% of what they *hear* and *see*	Watch moving picture	
	Watch exhibit	
	Watch demonstration	
70% of what they *say* or *write*	Do a site visit	Hearing, saying, seeing, and doing
90% of what they *say as they do a thing*	Do a dramatic presentation	
	Simulate a real experience	
	Do the real thing	

* Based on Edgar Dale, "Cone of Experience." (Adapted from *Audiovisual Methods in Teaching*, "Third Edition, Holt, Rinehart and Winston, Inc., 1969, p. 107).

Planning Staff Development

Supervision, when viewed by teachers as "for them," is the most powerful staff development tool available to supervisors. Staff who experience a high level of sincere, ongoing support are more likely to meet the high expectations set for them in a quality early childhood program. Unfortunately, supervisors are often challenged to overcome a common belief that supervision is punitive and deficit-based. Most people expect supervisors to come in, tell them what's wrong, pad it with a few positive comments, and then leave.

Effective staff development is based on trust. Establishing a trusting relationship in a supportive environment is the first step in achieving the goal of a highly competent staff that can implement a quality program. Supervisors create a relationship of trusting support when they convey clear expectations, develop individualized training plans for each staff member, offer honest feedback through observation and open communication, and provide consistent coaching. Staff then know that the supervisor's job is to help them be successful.

Clarifying Your Expectations

If you are clear about what you want to see happening in the classrooms you supervise, as well as what you will not tolerate, you are more likely to communicate your expectations clearly to your staff. Think about your "bottom line": what **must** happen and what **cannot** happen in the classrooms you supervise. Put on this list only those things that are very important to you and that you are willing to take a stand on.

A group of Head Start education coordinators attending a training session on the *Creative Curriculum* created a joint statement of their "Bottom Line" in order to more effectively convey clear expectations to their staff.

THE BOTTOM LINE

<u>What **Must** Happen</u>	<u>What **Cannot** Happen</u>
• Children treated with respect and caring.	• Punitive discipline, physical or emotional.
• Use of children's names in conversation.	• "Time outs" of more than two minutes (if at all).
• Teachers actively working with children.	• Remarks or actions that damage a child's self-esteem.
• Respectful conversations with parents.	• Forcing of food or using food as a punishment.
• Children making choices.	• Inappropriate behavior on the part of adults.
• Teachers listening to children's needs.	• Socializing with adults while supervising children.
• Respect for others—teamwork.	• Commercial posters on the walls.
• Flexibility and responsiveness.	• Unsafe environment.
• Limit setting.	• Unnecessary clutter.
• Appropriate materials.	• Long waits.
• Child-centered activities.	
• Attention to safety.	
• Children engaged and self-directed.	
• Children's work displayed.	
• Evidence of what children are learning.	
• Clean, organized room arrangement.	
• Conversation or productive "buzz."	

Staff members have a right to know exactly what job expectations you have established. Some programs use the Child Development Associate (CDA) Competencies to prepare job descriptions and design staff development. Another approach is to define the knowledge and skills needed to effectively implement the curriculum you use.

The Self-Assessment and Observation Form (included in Appendix A) identifies specific job expectations for implementing *The Creative Curriculum for Early Childhood*. This form is designed to be used by an individual teacher and her/his supervisor in planning staff development. Job expectations are organized under the following headings:

- Organizing the Environment
- Planning an Appropriate Daily Program
- Using Transition Times for Learning
- Supporting Children's Socio-Emotional Development
- Extending Children's Thinking

- Promoting Children's Physical Development
- Individualizing the Program
- The Block Corner
- The House Corner
- The Table Toy Area
- The Art Area
- Sand and Water
- The Library Corner
- Music and Movement
- Cooking
- Computers
- Outdoors
- Involving Parents in the Program

The process begins with a self-assessment that asks teachers to think about each of the job expectations and assign a rating on how highly they *value* it and to what extent they *demonstrate* the knowledge or skill. After completing the self-assessment part of the process, the supervisor and teacher decide on a date for an observation. More than one observation may be required to complete all of the items on the form.

If you decide to use the *Creative Curriculum* Self-Assessment and Observation Form as the basis for planning staff development, recognize that YOUR evaluation of the staff's needs may not coincide with THEIR perceived needs. However, staff development efforts will be more likely to succeed if they are planned around the declared needs of individual staff members, and what they value most.

Developing an Individual Training Plan

The most effective individual training plans focus first on job expectations that the staff member values highly but acknowledges he or she does not demonstrate adequately. Using the Self-Assessment and Observation Form as a guide, work with each teacher to design a plan, recognizing and building on individual interests and talents.

Begin the discussion by ensuring that each staff member is aware of the program's vision for children and families. Ask for and obtain their commitment to this vision of quality. Explain that the purpose of the self-assessment process is not to judge but to make a realistic determination of each person's individual areas of strength as well as needs. The more accurately the self-assessment reflects true levels of competence and areas of need, the more helpful you can be in planning support and assistance to promote individual growth.

Each training plan will be unique. Even when people are working on the same behaviors, training and support may be addressed differently. For example, a staff member who lacks knowledge in a particular area would need to read, or attend a class. Another person might understand the concept, but not see how to implement it; that training objective could include a visit to another classroom, or a brainstorming session with some colleagues. Yet another person might recognize that a problem exists and not know why. This individual's training plan could include a request for an observation to focus exclusively on the stated behavior. When there is agreement on objectives and strategies for achieving this, a written plan is developed which clearly states who will do what and by when. The planning process is on-going. At each step the plan can be reviewed, and revised, adjusting to the staff member's abilities, interests, and goals.

Of course there are times when staff will be grouped by interests or needs. Several staff who are working on the same topic can come together for a workshop, or just to share. Individualized staff training does not meet all of a person's training needs. It is still necessary to offer new ideas and information to staff, and to provide hands on training in all areas of the curriculum.

Individualizing staff development is consistent with developmentally appropriate practice and the philosophy of the *Creative Curriculum*. There are expectations within a framework, and skills and concepts are integrated by content that is meaningful to individuals in the group. All of us learn by constructing our own knowledge.

Observing and Recording Teacher Behaviors

Observation of teachers is an effective way to support staff as they travel towards competence. Objective observations will help supervisors and staff members determine strengths as well as training needs. The observations should be jointly planned and are most helpful when the focus is on a goal the teacher has identified. For example, instead of looking for all the reasons that a large group time isn't working, the purpose of an observation might be to develop strategies for a meaningful and well-organized large group activity. The intention here is to help the teacher look at what she/he can do to achieve the goal, instead of constantly looking at what is missing. Video taping is an excellent method of self observation. We don't have many opportunities to see ourselves objectively. It is a powerful learning experience.

Observations will provide you with objective information about each person's strengths and needs that can then be used to support the achievement of identified goals. Observation data that are useful must meet the following criteria:

- **Objectivity:** Include only the facts about what happens, not labels, judgments, or inferences drawn. Record only what the teacher does and says and what the children do and say in response.

- **Specificity:** Record as much information as possible to present a picture of the teacher's actions. Include details such as the number of children/adults involved, where in the room the action is taking place, words and tone of voice used, and so on.

- **Accuracy:** Record the teacher's and children's words and actions directly and in the order in which they happen. Try to include direct quotations whenever possible.

- **Completeness:** Include descriptions of activities from beginning to end. Record information about the setting (where in the room or outdoor area the action is taking place), what the teacher does, the teacher's words (if any), and the children's response.

Observation Methods

A number of methods for recording observations can be used. Supervisors use notebooks, stenograph pads, index cards, and observation forms. There are benefits and drawbacks to any method. Therefore, investigate the alternatives by talking with other supervisors and staff you will be observing, experimenting on your own, and finally recognizing what your goals for observation are and how they can best be achieved.

Several forms are included for use in supporting teachers on implementing the *Creative Curriculum*. (All staff development forms can be found in Appendix B.) The "Observation of the Environment" form has spaces on which you can record descriptions of the general layout of the classroom and the organization of the indoor and outdoor areas. The "Teacher Observation" form helps you organize the observation around the stated goal. In the box marked "Goal," you clearly define how you and the teacher would like things to be. Where it says "Setting," note the area and activity you are observing. Under the category "Teacher," you record specifically what the teacher does and says. The "Outcome" is what follows the incident—how the children or another adult respond to the teacher's actions. The "Comments" section allows you to record notes to yourself or questions you might want to ask the teacher as a result of the observation. The information is best utilized when you and the teacher keep referring to the goal and asking, "How did this interaction either support or not support the attainment of my goal?"

As children arrive, you can begin recording the teacher's interactions with children and other adults, and the children's use of the environment. Remember that your task is to record what is happening and to be as unobtrusive as possible. Certainly you will want to talk with the children as they come up to you; they will undoubtedly ask what you are doing. Politely inform them that you are writing down what is happening in their room and outdoors, speak with them briefly, and return to your task.

Use a form such as the "Observation Summary" to list the strengths you observed and your recommendations to the teacher. This form, along with your observation record, should be given to the teacher immediately after the observation. People are naturally curious about what you have written about them and their class. Plan a feedback conference with the teacher the same day.

The Feedback Conference

The feedback conference is part of the cycle of on-going coaching and support. Since its primary function is to enable the teacher to achieve her/his staff development goals, it is less likely to be threatening when it is a regular component of coaching received by the teacher and when it focuses on how she/he can achieve the goals.

Although each feedback conference will be somewhat different, there are several strategies that may be helpful in conducting these sessions.

- **Schedule the conference the same day or as close to your observation as possible.** Even though you have recorded most of the information you will discuss, you and the teacher will still rely to some extent on your memories for details. Conduct the conference while the events are fresh for both of you.

- **Be descriptive, not interpretive.** Identify for the teacher your perceptions of what he or she did and said while interacting with children or working with parents. Use terms that are objective and avoid using labels and judgmental phrases. For example, you could state, "I noticed that you described Jenny's block construction by talking about the shapes she used and how she used them," instead of "your language with children is good."

- **Be specific, not general.** Tell the teacher in as much detail as possible what you saw and heard during an observation. For example, you could state, "You were calm but firm when you helped Antonio to stop pulling Keshia's hair," instead of "you break up fights well."

- **Ask the teacher to describe what he or she did and the reasons for the behavior.** The teacher's perceptions of his or her performance are valuable, and the opportunity for voicing those perceptions should be encouraged especially if the teacher has done something you regard as inappropriate. For example, you could ask a teacher why she read a particular story, selected certain helpers to set the table for mealtime, or asked a certain child if the floor was smooth or rough.

- **Direct the feedback toward the teacher's goals.** Staying goal focused will be less confrontational and will help to build the teacher's self-esteem and a commitment to development. For example, if the teacher's goal was to talk to children in ways that build self-esteem, you might make the following observations: "Pete smiled at you when you thanked him for sharing the markers," or, "Jodie looked at the floor and twisted her hair when you said 'How many times have I told you not to sit on the table.' What else might you have said?"

- **If possible, provide feedback in response to specific requests.** Feedback is most useful when the receiver has specifically asked for assistance in a particular area.

- **Give no more feedback than the person can absorb.** If a teacher asks how he/she is doing in a specific area, confine your comments to that specific area. Offering feedback about additional observations can overwhelm and confuse the teacher.

- **End the conference with an action plan.** Review identified strengths and needs. Use a form such as the "Staff Development Worksheet" to write a plan together. You and the teacher would identify what job behavior(s) will be the focus of staff development efforts and what goals the teacher wants to set. Each plan specifies what they will do and by what date. Before concluding the conference, the date for the next observation is set. For example, suppose that a teacher wants to organize the environment to better promote physical development. Based on your observation, you note that she has included a number of opportunities for children to develop large and small muscles. Her focus for the next two weeks might be to provide more opportunities for children to use all their senses to explore and understand. You and the teacher could brainstorm about several activities, such as using canisters with different spices and herbs in them, tasting trays with raw vegetables, and "feely" bags with natural materials. You might offer to provide several resource books to help the teacher identify additional activities. You will focus your observations on the activities to meet this objective during your next visit, three weeks later.

Challenging Conferences

The feedback conference can be particularly challenging when you have identified a real problem you must discuss with a teacher. The challenge is to present your concerns in a way that the teacher will accept your observations and assessment and be willing to make an effort to change. In these situations, it is especially important to be well prepared for the feedback conference. Take time to review your notes. Identify areas of strength as well as any concerns you have identified. Consider what might be behind a teacher's actions. We want teachers to think about the causes for a child's misbehavior, and we should be willing to do the same for a teacher. Thinking about the reasons for a teacher's inappropriate practices will help you to identify an approach that is more likely to be successful. Decide what is most important to address at the feedback conference. If you have too long a list of concerns, you will face a very defensive teacher. Keep in mind that your goal as a supervisor is to promote growth, not to force change. The exception to this is when a teacher's practices are completely inappropriate and harmful to children. In these situations, you have to be very clear about what must change immediately.

How you actually handle the feedback conference will depend on your communication style and what you know about the person you have observed. Often it is helpful to pose questions to encourage the teacher's active participation. Here is one example of how a feedback conference might proceed.

- **Open the conference by showing you appreciate how the teacher might be feeling:** "I can see it was a trying day today," or "This is the first time I've had a chance to observe in your room and I'm sure you felt a little apprehensive."

- **Pose a question to involve the teacher:** "How do you feel the day went?"

- **Use objective notes to help the teacher become aware of what actually happened:** "Let's look at the notes I took and see what they tell us."

- **Encourage awareness:** "Did you notice that...?" or "What do you think about what happened?"

- **Discuss the teacher's intentions:** "What did you hope would happen?" or "I was wondering if you intended...?"

- **Look at alternatives with the teacher:** "I wonder what would have happened if you had tried...." or "Have you ever tried ...?" or "There may be another way to achieve your objectives and avoid the problem you ran into. It might work if you try...."

- **Provide perspective on the situation so the teacher can see the bigger picture.** For example, discuss the overall goals of the program, share the NAEYC publication on *Developmentally Appropriate Practice* or the *Head Start Program Performance Standards*.

- **Identify specific steps to work on and offer support.** Arrange a follow-up observation and conference to continue your support.

This section has presented information on how to plan for staff development. The following chapter addresses another aspect of staff development, classroom visits—what to look for and why it is important.

III. Classroom Visits

The best way to support teachers in implementing the *Creative Curriculum* is to visit their classrooms and provide technical assistance. Classroom visits enable you to see where each teaching team is succeeding or encountering difficulties so that you can target your assistance and support. In visiting classrooms, you will want to focus your attention on specific program areas that are critical to implementing the *Creative Curriculum*. These include the following:

- the physical environment of the classroom and outdoor areas;

- equipment and materials that teachers have selected and displayed;

- the program structure, including the daily schedule and routines;

- the activities and experiences that teachers provide for the children;

- the quality of interactions and how teachers support social development;

- the staff's ability to individualize the program; and

- the extent of parent involvement in the program.

This chapter of the *Guide* discusses each of the seven program areas listed above. It illustrates what you should see and why, identifies warning signs that indicate teachers are encountering difficulties, and suggests strategies for working with staff to improve the program.

The Environment

The first step in implementing the *Creative Curriculum* is to divide the physical environment into interest areas. The areas that are included in the *Creative Curriculum* are blocks, house corner, art, table toys, sand and water, library, music and movement, cooking, computers, and outdoors. The environment should be well organized and planned to support positive interactions and to meet individual and group needs. You can provide teachers with much-needed support by noting any problems they are having that may be caused by the arrangement of the physical environment and by providing practical suggestions for making improvements.

WHAT YOU SHOULD SEE	WHY
Clearly defined interest areas that accommodate one to five children.	Young children work best in small groups where they can learn to relate to other children, establish friendships, and solve problems together.
Use of low furniture to define areas, allowing teachers to see into all areas while at the same time giving children a sense of privacy.	Use of low furniture to define work spaces helps children concentrate because they are not distracted by activities in other areas. At the same time, teachers can see the children to ensure their safety.
Areas set up for different kinds of activities: dramatic play, art, blocks, table toys, books, sand and water, and large muscle activities.	An important goal of early childhood education is to help children learn to make their own choices. In order to do this, the choices must be obvious to them.

Noisy areas separated from quiet areas; for example, the house corner and block corner should be located together, separated from the library and table toys areas.

Children will be better able to focus on activities and less distracted.

Materials displayed on low shelves where children can reach what they need.

When the materials are readily accessible, children learn to take responsibility for their environment and develop self-esteem.

Private hideaways and soft spaces where children can relax and be alone or with a friend (e.g., large pillows, rugs, rocking chairs, platforms, couches).

Children who spend long hours in a group environment need a place to relax that is soft and comforting. This is very important for their mental health and promotes positive behavior.

Materials displayed on shelves near where they will be used, and picture labels showing where each object belongs.

Logical grouping of materials promotes their appropriate use. Labeling the place for each object helps children maintain the environment and conveys the message that order is valued.

Pictures on the walls at the children's eye level; their work attractively displayed as well as selected pictures relevant to the children's interests.

Children will not notice walls covered with pictures that are far above their eye level. Displaying their work conveys respect for their efforts.

Warning Signs That the Environment Is Not Working

Children's behavior is a clue to assessing the appropriateness of the environment. You should work with the staff to assess the environment and consider making changes if you observe children doing the following:

- consistently running in the classroom;
- wandering around looking for things to do;
- repeating the same activity over and over again;
- remaining uninvolved and unable to stick with an activity;
- fighting over toys and materials;
- using materials destructively;
- shouting from one area to the next—creating a high noise level;
- crawling under tables or on shelves;
- resisting cleaning up; and
- consistently depending on adults for the things they need.

Although these behaviors may have a variety of causes, the physical environment must also be considered in assessing how to deal with behavior that is not conducive to learning. In working with teachers on improving their environment, first consider *why* they may have organized the room inappropriately. Listed below are some examples of inappropriate environments for young children and the reasons that teachers may have had for organizing the environment in these ways.

WARNING SIGNS	WHY THIS MIGHT BE HAPPENING
Shelves and furniture are arranged against the wall leaving open spaces that encourage children to run.	Teachers sometimes do this if the room is small, with the idea of giving children more space. They may feel it is the only way for them to see all the children at once.
Walls are cluttered with too many pictures far above the children's eye level.	Teachers may have used their own height to determine where to put displays. They may feel that lots of pictures make the room more attractive.
Toys are not attractively displayed or organized.	Teachers may feel that the children use toys all day and therefore clean-up before the end of the day is a waste of time.
The same materials are out day after day and the children are bored with them.	Teachers may feel they don't have the time to rotate materials or the resources to acquire new ones.
There are no soft areas where children can get away and be by themselves.	Teachers sometimes use only what is provided in the room and don't consider it their role to create new spaces or add to the environment.

Strategies for Working with Teachers on the Environment

- Use an environmental rating scale to evaluate the classroom and share results with the staff.

- Observe children's behavior and identify ways in which the environment may be supporting and encouraging this behavior.

- Discuss your observations with the teaching team and encourage them to share how they are feeling about any problems you have noted.

- Show the slide/videotape *The New Room Arrangement as a Teaching Strategy* and discuss how the information presented can be used to improve the classrooms.

- Help teachers identify specific changes they'd like to try, and plan a work session to implement the changes.

Equipment and Materials

The success of each interest area in the *Creative Curriculum* depends on the selection and display of the equipment and materials that are housed in each area. There should be a rich supply of materials that are rotated and replaced often enough to maintain children's interest and continually challenge them. If you see the same materials displayed in an interest area on every visit, materials that are not developmentally appropriate, or poorly organized displays, this should alert you to a need to work with the teachers in that classroom on equipment and materials. To assist teachers in providing a rich assortment of appropriate materials, offer suggestions of what should be available in each interest area. Listed below, by interest area, are suggested materials for implementing the *Creative Curriculum*.

Furniture

- Solid colored carpeting
- Storage shelves (5-6)
- Book display shelf
- Plastic basins for storage
- Child-size tables and chairs
- Adult rocking chair
- Bean bag chairs

Block Corner
- Complete set of hardwood unit blocks (approximately 300-400 pieces for 10 to 15 children)
- Hollow blocks
- Carpet—solid color and tight weave
- People props
    multi-ethnic family sets
    set of multi-ethnic wooden community helpers
- Animal props (farm and/or zoo animals)
- Transportation props
    selection of large and small cars, trucks, fire engines, trains, buses, airplanes set of traffic signs
- Doll house furniture
    beds, chairs, tables (at least 2 of each)
- Decorative items
    set of colored cube blocks
    assorted objects such as shells, carpet samples, popsicle sticks, tiles

House Corner

- Table and 4 chairs
- High chair
- Doll bed
- Stove
- Refrigerator
- Sink
- Baby dolls (multi-ethnic)
- Doll clothes and blankets
- Pots, pans, and utensils
- Broom and/or mop
- Mirror—full length
- Dishes
- Books and magazines

- Telephone
- Male and female dress-up clothes
- Hats
- Costume jewelry
- Pocketbooks and/or suitcases
- Prop boxes for themes (barber shop, grocery store, etc.)

Table Toys

- Puzzles (wooden, rubber inserts, cardboard)
- Sewing cards and yarn
- Legos
- Lotto games
- Beads for stringing
- Pegs and pegboard
- Colored inch-cube blocks
- Parquetry or pattern blocks
- Interlocking toys
- Stacking rings and/or nesting cubes (2)
- Simple games (memory, color matching games)
- Attribute blocks
- Objects to sniff, smell, and taste (cinnamon, onions, coffee, lemon/orange peels, nutmeg, cloves)
- Objects to feel and sort and classify (shells, stones, pebbles, seeds, nuts, leaves)
- Collectibles (buttons, bottle caps, keys, shells)
- Cuisenaire rods
- Unifix cubes
- Table blocks (hardwood)
- Self-help skill frames (buttoning, zipping, tying)
- Dramatic play props (doll house furniture, small family set and animals)

Art Area

- Easels—2 sided with paint wells
- Tempera paints (primary colors: red, blue, yellow, white and black)
- Brushes—wooden handles with 1" and 1/4" bristles
- Paper: newsprint, manila drawing paper, colored construction paper
- Glue and/or paste
- White and colored chalk
- Large crayons
- Water-based magic markers
- Safety scissors for left- and right-handed children
- Finger paint (homemade or purchased) and paper
- Trays for finger painting
- Clay (plasticine and water-based)
- Ingredients for playdough
- Smocks (donated old shirts or plastic smocks)
- Yarn (assorted colors and thicknesses)
- Tagboard or cardboard, or styrofoam trays
- Hole punchers
- Stapler and staples
- Collectibles for collages and construction
- Clean-up supplies—sponges, buckets, liquid soap
- Old tablecloth or plastic for floor covering

Library

- Rocking chair, soft chair, mattress, and/or pillows
- Carpeted floor
- Book stand in which displayed book covers face the viewer
- Books about feelings and attitudes
- Books about family and friends
- Books about everyday living experiences
- Books about science and nature
- Books about fun and fantasy
- Homemade books
- Puppets
- Flannel board and story cutouts
- Writing tools (pencils, crayons, chalk, magic markers)
- Printing tools (stamps and ink pads)
- Paper (computer printout paper, index cards)
- Tools (scissors, hole punch, stapler)

Sand and Water Area

- Sand/water play table or basins
- Sand or water play props: measuring cups, funnels, magnifying glasses, ping-pong balls, shells, cookie cutters, shovels, spoons, squirt bottles, basters (all plastic)
- Plastic smocks for water play
- Buckets, sponges, brooms, and mops for clean-up

Woodworking

- Woodworking bench or flat tree stump
- Real tools (hammer, saws, vise, chisel, screwdrivers, hand drill, pliers)
- Nails, screws, ruler, carpenter's pencil, corks
- Hard and soft wood scraps and boards
- Wood glue

Music and Movement

- Record player, tape recorder
- Instruments for adults to play (piano, autoharp, guitar)
- Homemade and commercial rhythm band instruments (drums, triangles)
- Scarves, streamers, balloons
- Folk music albums/tapes
- Exercise movement albums/tapes
- Classical albums/tapes
- Story tapes
- Quiet music albums/tapes
- Teacher song books/finger play books

Cooking

- Electric burner (double)
- Plastic bowls (various sizes)
- Plastic measuring spoons
- Plastic measuring cups
- Pyrex measuring cups

- Wooden spoons
- Funnels
- Wire whisk
- Egg beater
- Potato masher
- Colander
- Sifter
- Pastry brushes
- Paring knives
- Plastic knives
- Cutting board
- Spatulas
- Vegetable peelers
- Strawberry hullers
- Hand grinder
- Candy thermometer
- Juicers
- Can openers
- Pitchers
- Rolling pin
- Ladle
- Cookie cutters
- Tongs
- Cheesecloth
- Pastry bag
- Large aprons
- Cookie sheets
- Muffin tin
- Round cake pans
- Oblong cake pan
- Saucepans with lids
- Cooking shears
- Ice cream freezer
- Trivets
- Pot holders
- Grater
- Sponges

Computer Area

- Macintosh II LC School computer, IBM or IBM-compatible computer or Commodore with monitor
- Printer
- T-switch for printer
- Computer cables
- Surge protector
- Software (use the list in the *Creative Curriculum* or select from the following):
    - Gertrude's Secrets (The Learning Company)
    - Moptown's Parade (The Learning Company)
    - What Makes a Dinosaur Soar? (D.C. Heath)
    - The Playroom (Broderbund)
    - Magic Slate (Sunburst)
    - Color Me! (Visual Learning System)
    - Colors and Shapes (Hartley)
    - Muppetville (Sunburst)

      A Great Leap (D.C. Heath)
      McGee (Lawrence Productions)
      Stickybear Reading (Weekly Reader)
      Words and Concepts (Learner Systems)
      Muppets on Stage (Sunburst)

- Computer paper
- Software disk storage boxes
- Blank diskettes

Outdoor Area

- Swings, slides, climbers
- Tricycles, wheelbarrows, wagons
- Balls (several sizes) and bats
- Sandbox area with sand, shovels, buckets, spoons, bowls, gelatin molds, plastic bottles cut in half, funnels, etc.
- Containers for water play, pails and buckets, large house-painting brushes for water play
- Large boxes
- Tires, boards, sawhorses
- Garden tools, rakes, and shovels
- Jump ropes, hoops

In visiting the classrooms you supervise, you have many opportunities to help teachers assess the equipment and materials they have selected and displayed for children. Listed below are examples of what you should see and why each is important to implementing the *Creative Curriculum*.

WHAT YOU SHOULD SEE	WHY
Materials and equipment appropriate for the age and stage of development of the children in the room.	Children should experience success and at the same time be sufficiently challenged to learn new skills and concepts.
Materials relevant to the cultural backgrounds and life experiences of the children.	Children need familiar materials before they are asked to learn new concepts. Cultural relevancy is important for identity and self-esteem.
Materials and equipment in good repair with no sharp edges, peeling paint, or splinters.	For safety reasons, all materials and equipment must be in top repair at all times.
Sufficient quantities of materials and multiple sets when possible.	Young children are better able to share materials when they have first experienced having enough.
Materials in each interest area that reflect the curriculum and specific interests of the children (e.g., if the children have been visiting a construction site near the center, teachers might add hard hats and lunch pails to the house corner; wires, pipes, and construction vehicles to the block area; and books on buildings to the library corner).	Children learn by interacting with real objects and recreating what they have experienced. Materials in each interest area should reflect the children's experiences and interests.
Materials that vary in complexity (e.g., 5-piece puzzles as well as 10- and 12-piece puzzles, playdough, and a box of utensils for children to use if they wish).	Children of similar ages can be at very different stages of development. Materials and equipment should allow all children to experience success.
Material displays with picture labels to show where each object or set of objects belongs when not in use.	Displays tell children that everything has a place and helps them find and return materials when they are finished. Clean-up becomes a self-correcting matching game.
Toys with small pieces stored in dishpans or containers that enable children to reach what they need.	Appropriate storage containers allow children to find what they need without having to spill everything out.
Materials that are used together, grouped together.	Grouping together all materials that are used together tells children how materials are to be used and what goes together.

Materials that are nonsexist (e.g., men's dress-up clothes in the house corner; community helpers showing men and women in all roles in the block area; books and pictures showing women in leadership roles and men in nurturing roles) and multiethnic.

Nonsexist materials help children learn that boys and girls can assume nurturing roles in the family as well as a wide range of jobs and professions. Materials that reflect various cultures help children develop self-esteem and appreciation for others.

Soft materials as well as hard ones (e.g., pillows, dough, fingerpaint, clay, sand and water).

Soft materials are relaxing and soothing to children. This is especially important for young children in day care for long hours.

Warning Signs That Materials and Equipment Are Inappropriate

Several warning signs can alert you to the need to work with staff on the selection and display of materials and equipment. By considering the possible causes for these signals, you can identify strategies for improving the situation.

WARNING SIGNS

WHY THIS MIGHT BE HAPPENING

Children depend on adults to complete tasks they start and appear frustrated when they can't get immediate assistance.

The materials selected may be too difficult for the children to handle on their own.

Children don't clean up materials when they are finished. At clean-up time, materials are placed anywhere in the room.

Children may not know where things go because there are no labels to identify specified places for materials.

Boys tend to ignore the house corner and girls are rarely seen in the block corner or large muscle area.

The messages conveyed by the equipment and materials in these areas may be sexist.

Children do the same things over and over, using materials in a repetitive way and losing interest quickly.

The materials may not be complex enough to maintain interest (e.g., new utensils may be needed in the water table or new props in the block area).

Children are constantly fighting over materials and toys.

Teachers may be requiring too much sharing when they could provide multiple sets of materials as well as more choices that interest the children.

Strategies for Working with Staff

- Review the basic equipment and materials list with the staff and discuss what items they have in each interest area and where they might get others that are needed.

- Share any warning signs you have noted; discuss the possible causes and what could be done to address the problems.

- Assist teachers in reorganizing the display of materials to make them more attractive and logical to children.

- Hold a workshop to make materials and labels for the classroom.

Program Structure: Schedule and Routines

Every classroom should have a schedule posted that defines the daily program. The sample schedule in the *Creative Curriculum* (Setting the Stage) can be adapted to meet the specific requirements of your program. Young children feel more comfortable when there is a consistent schedule and set of routines that they follow each day. Attention to daily routines such as meal times, naptime, and transition periods can make the daily program run more smoothly.

WHAT YOU SHOULD SEE	WHY
Clearly defined periods of the day, from the opening of the center to the departure of the last child.	All adults in the classroom, including substitutes, should know the daily schedule and be able to follow a consistent sequence of activities.
A balance of active and quiet times during the day.	Young children need lots of active play but they also tire easily. The schedule should reflect a good balance of both kinds of activity periods.
Many opportunities for children to be in small groups.	Young children learn best in small group activities rather than in a large group where they can't be actively involved and are required to sit still.
Provision for children to play outdoors at least twice during the day.	Children need fresh air and a place to run, jump, and play actively.
Sufficient time allocated for transitions and routines such as clean-up, hand washing, teeth brushing, and preparation for lunch.	Routines are important learning times, and children should not be rushed through these periods of the day.
Time periods appropriate to the developmental abilities of the children (e.g., preschoolers cannot be expected to sit still for 45 minutes of circle time).	Behavior problems can be averted by adjusting the schedule to the abilities of the children. Just because children will sit if we ask them to doesn't mean that they are learning from this activity.
Sufficient time allocated for children to select their own activities and play for an extended time (e.g., at least one hour of free play in the morning and in the afternoon).	Children learn best when they can select activities that interest them and when they have time to see a project through to completion. These are skills we want to encourage in early childhood.

Making Transitions and Routines Work

Transitions can often be unsettling times for young children. They are the in-between times when children are moving from one activity to the next—from clean-up to circle time, from outdoor play to lunch preparation and lunch time. They can become problem periods when children who have nothing to do choose to run around, take out toys that have already been put away, and generally be disruptive. Waiting is not easy for young children and when they are not purposefully occupied, they find something to do that may not fit in with the staff's plans.

Similarly, routines such as meal times and naptime are an important part of the daily program. Attention to making routines comfortable for children as well as times for learning can greatly enhance the program and make life easier for the staff.

WHAT YOU SHOULD SEE	WHY
Children given sufficient warning before a transition period to complete what they are doing and prepare for the next activity.	Young children respond better when they are not surprised by an immediate command to change what they are doing. They are more likely to cooperate when they have time to complete what they have started.
Teachers explaining what is coming next and what is expected (e.g., "In a few minutes we'll be getting ready for lunch. This means everyone will need to wash their hands.")	Children feel more in control when they know what is expected of them and why.
Children going in small groups to wash hands, prepare for outdoor time, and so on, rather than all going at once.	When children are in small groups, less waiting time is required.
Children meaningfully involved in transition activities such as washing paint brushes, setting tables for a meal, or preparing the cots for naptime.	These housekeeping chores are learning times for children and give them an important role in classroom maintenance.
A relaxed atmosphere at meal times. Children and adults engaged in conversations, with no one rushed or required to finish everything.	Children need time to digest their food in a calm environment and to learn about different foods. Many social skills can be acquired during meal times.
Children serving themselves family style and encouraged but not forced to try everything.	Serving themselves, children learn to judge how much they can eat, develop small muscle control, and develop self-esteem.

Warning Signs That the Program Structure Is Not Working

Observing in each classroom enables you to assess whether the program structure is working for or against the staff. If you note any of the warning signs listed below, consider the possible causes before designing approaches to working with teachers on the problems.

WARNING SIGNS	WHY THIS MIGHT BE HAPPENING
Children seem confused about where they are expected to be and what they are expected to be doing.	Teachers may be inconsistent in following the schedule and fail to help children learn the daily sequence of events.
Children can be found sitting for long periods of time (for example, at circle time).	Sometimes teachers think that circle time is the best time to teach children new skills and concepts. They do not understand how children learn through their involvement in each interest area.
Children are running a lot in the classroom and are having trouble getting involved in activities.	The schedule may not have a balance of active and quiet activities; the children need more time to run and use their large muscles.
Children are taken outside only in good weather. When it is cold, the outdoor period is shortened or eliminated.	Teachers do not always understand the importance of outdoor play for children's health and well-being. They fail to dress adequately for outdoors and become cold before the children do.
Teachers are constantly trying to get children to stay in line and be orderly as they go through daily routines. Children tend to wander away and have to be brought back to the group.	Transitions times are not planned for. Teachers sometimes try to get the whole group through a routine rather than divide them into small groups with each group meaningfully occupied.
During free play, teachers organize choices but do not actively interact with children or try to extend their play.	Teachers may not appreciate the value of free play as the principal learning time for young children.
Most of the routine tasks such as preparing tables for meals, setting out cots, and cleaning up are performed by adults while children wait.	Teachers sometimes fail to appreciate the learning opportunities for children in routines. In trying to be efficient and get routine tasks finished and out of the way, teachers assume all responsibilities themselves.
Teachers do not eat with the children. They serve children and expect them to clean their plates before asking for more.	Teachers may not view meal times as an important part of the program. They do not appreciate the learning opportunities and do not trust the children to serve themselves. They impose adult standards on the children, valuing neatness more than independence.

Strategies for Working with Staff

- Review the daily schedule posted in the classroom by the teachers and compare it to the criteria and the sample schedule in the *Creative Curriculum*. Observe how the schedule works for the children. Work with teachers to make adjustments if you note problems.

- Offer suggestions for making the outdoor period a meaningful learning time by dealing with problems that teachers identify (e.g., poor weather conditions, little to do outdoors).

- Identify problems that teachers may be having at transition times and offer suggestions for making these periods run more smoothly.

- Suggest that teachers illustrate the schedule with pictures to help children follow the sequence of each day.

- If children are required to sit in a group and listen for long periods of time, discuss how much more valuable active learning is for children and suggest more appropriate activity choices.

Activities and Experiences[2]

In the *Creative Curriculum*, the activities and experiences planned for children should be **age appropriate** as well as **individually appropriate**. Age appropriateness is based on a recognition that children grow and develop in predictable stages. All children pass through the same stages in all areas of development: physical, emotional, social, and cognitive. For example, children participate in parallel play activities before they can successfully play cooperatively with other children. Children scribble before they draw recognizable shapes and representational pictures. Jumping in place precedes hopping on one foot. Children can identify concrete objects before they can understand abstract concepts.

Activities and experiences are individually appropriate if they are based on an understanding that children are individuals who grow and develop at their own rate. No two children are likely to be at the same stage in all areas of development at a given time. The ability to recognize where each child is in his/her development, and to appreciate the unique interests and concerns of each child, enables staff to plan activities that are individually appropriate.

In planning activities for all interest areas, teachers should be guided by an understanding of how children learn. The following principles can be used as guidelines in designing activities.

- Socio-emotional development is closely tied to cognitive development. Children must feel secure in the environment and good about themselves if they are to learn and grow optimally.

- Children learn best through their active interactions with people and objects in their immediate environment. They explore, try out ideas, see what happens,

---

2   Parts of this section are based on a chapter developed by this author in *A Guide for Education Coordinators in Head Start* (Washington, DC: U.S. Department of Health and Human Services, Office of Human Development Services, Administration for Children, Youth and Families, 1986), p. 50, and on criteria in Sue Bredekamp (ed.), *Developmentally Appropriate Practice* (Washington, DC: NAEYC, 1987), pp. 54-57.

and attempt to make sense of the results based on the knowledge they already have.

- New experiences, skills, and information should be closely related to what children already know and what they can do.

- Activities and experiences should begin with the simple and move to the more complex, from the concrete to the more abstract.

- Children use their whole bodies and their senses in learning about the world around them.

- When children can select their own activities and their choices are respected, they tend to select activities that are appropriate for their abilities and that maintain their interest and involvement.

When you observe in the classrooms you supervise, you should see children actively engaged in activities that are inherently of interest to them. Listed below are some examples of what you should see during an observation and why these kinds of activities and experiences are important for children's growth.

WHAT YOU SHOULD SEE	WHY
Children working in small groups on individual or self-selected activities.	Young children learn best in small groups where they can actively engage in interactions with peers on tasks that interest them.
Children acquiring concepts and skills through meaningful activities such as playing with blocks, measuring sand and water, sorting and classifying materials, drawing and painting, and observing changes around them.	Learning takes place when children have a chance to try out their ideas and see for themselves the results of their actions.
Activities planned each day to allow children to use large muscles freely (e.g., jumping, running, climbing).	Physical and mental health and development depend on opportunities to continually practice new skills and refine them.
Activities planned for children to develop small muscle skills (e.g., placing pegs in a board, cutting, painting, constructing with small blocks).	Development of small muscles is a prerequisite to writing and other refined tasks.
Children engaged in activities that enable them to represent their ideas (e.g., using art materials, telling stories, participating in dramatic play).	In representing their ideas, children are learning to think abstractly and preparing for reading. In order to read, children must understand that words represent ideas.

Many opportunities for children to learn that reading and writing have meaning (e.g., a rich assortment of books, regular story times in the schedule and during free play, use of charts in the room).

Children will be motivated to read and write if they understand that words have meaning. Teaching letters and numbers before children have acquired this understanding is inappropriate.

Teachers continually observing children and interacting as appropriate to facilitate children's use of materials; adding new materials when needed; and making suggestions to extend children's play.

Teaching young children means guiding and facilitating their learning, not telling them the answers or what to do.

Questions designed to encourage children to think and express their ideas; teachers accepting more than one right answer and encouraging creative thinking.

An important goal of early childhood education is to help children develop self-confidence as learners and to promote creative thinking. If children know their responses will be respected, they are more willing to freely share their ideas.

Children engaged in project work, cooperating on a common goal (e.g., making a mural, planning an event, recreating a city in the block corner, studying a topic in depth, preparing a meal).

Working together, children learn to respect the ideas of others, to contribute to a joint effort, and to develop social skills.

Teacher-directed activities involving children in small groups on a task such as making playdough, planting seeds, or playing a classification game.

There should be a balance of child-initiated and adult-initiated activities. What is important is that children are actively involved.

Warning Signs That the Activities Are Inappropriate

When you make classroom observations, you may not see children and teachers actively involved in activities as described above. There are several warning signs that should make you question whether the activities the teachers have planned and implemented are developmentally appropriate.

WARNING SIGNS

WHY THIS MIGHT BE HAPPENING

Activities planned focus entirely on cognitive tasks and rote learning, with little consideration for socio-emotional and physical needs.

Teachers may feel that school is for learning and that cognitive development is most important. They feel most comfortable in a teaching role.

All children are expected to complete the same tasks together.

This way of structuring activities is similar to the school experiences of the teachers, and they believe it is appropriate for young children.

Most activities are directed by teachers for the whole group. Children are expected to sit quietly and follow directions.	Teachers may feel that they are preparing children for school in this way.
Art activities tend to be product oriented. Teachers prepare cut shapes for the children to use in prescribed ways.	The product may be more valued than the process. Teachers may want the children to have something to show their parents and to display in the room.
Ditto sheets and workbooks are used to help children learn skills and concepts.	These activities keep children quiet. Adults mistakenly believe that children will learn from ditto sheets.
Activities stress academic learning such as recognizing and writing the alphabet and numbers or coloring within the lines.	It is easier for teachers to design these kinds of activities than to plan for children's active learning.
Children are required to sit quietly and listen in a group, raise their hands if they have something to say, and take turns giving answers to questions posed by the teachers.	Teachers may feel that this is appropriate behavior for children who will soon be going to elementary school.

Strategies for Working with Staff on Appropriate Activities

- Show the videotape *The Creative Curriculum* to illustrate how children learn in each interest area through active play.

- Share with staff the NAEYC publication on *Developmentally Appropriate Practice* and post the chart that compares appropriate and inappropriate practice for the relevant age group.

- Use examples from the sections in each module of the *Creative Curriculum* on the teacher's role to help teachers plan appropriate activities and experiences.

- Help teachers look at the environment as the focus for planning appropriate activities and experiences.

- Work with teachers to design activities and experiences that meet the criteria for developmental appropriateness.

- Plan teacher-led workshops to help parents understand the value of children learning through active involvement with materials and people.

Supportive Interactions and Positive Social Development

The quality of the program and the success of the curriculum depend to a great extent on the interactions that take place between adults and children. In a developmentally appropriate program, teachers respond to the children in ways that demonstrate a knowledge of their stage of development and an appreciation of individual needs.

The atmosphere in the room reflects the quality of the interactions. Lively chatter can be heard as children talk and work together and adults react to children's ideas, questions, and concerns. Teachers are genuinely interested in what children are doing, how they are feeling, and what they have to say. Teacher expectations reflect a recognition of what children can realistically understand and do at their stage of development. Cooperation and real caring among children and between children and adults are evident.

WHAT YOU SHOULD SEE	WHY
Teachers responding to children's needs and questions quickly and positively; distressed children being comforted and helped to deal with problems constructively.	Children develop a sense of trust and self-esteem when adults are responsive to their needs. They learn that they are important and worthy people.
Teachers kneeling down when talking to a child to establish eye contact.	Eye contact promotes good communication. Children feel more respected when adults are at their level.
Teachers demonstrating respect for children's feelings and ideas.	Each individual child's feelings are real for him or her. When adults convey respect, a child's self-esteem grows.
Teachers stating what they want to see happening, not just the behavior they want stopped.	Stating desired behaviors gives children constructive feedback on what they can do as well as what is not acceptable.
Teachers establishing clear rules and limits for behavior and applying them consistently and calmly.	Children respond better when they know what is expected and when they feel the rules are enforced fairly.
Teachers helping children resolve conflicts and learn to work out solutions to their problems.	Problem solving is an important social and cognitive skill for children to develop. The ability to work out solutions to problems builds self-esteem.
Reinforcement of cooperative behavior; children encouraged to work together and to care for one another.	When children acquire skills in working with others, their self-esteem grows and they exhibit fewer behavior problems.
Children helped to understand other points of view and to accept individual differences.	The ability to see things from another perspective is an important cognitive skill and critical to living successfully in a group.

Teachers providing encouragement and suggestions to enable children to solve problems on their own, complete a challenging task, and learn from their mistakes.

When so encouraged, children gain confidence, self-esteem, and a deeper understanding of new concepts.

Teachers making sure that every child has a friend and supporting each child's efforts to renegotiate friendships when necessary.

The ability to make friends and renegotiate friendships is a skill central to children's mental health. Children who leave the preschool years feeling friendless are likely to experience social and learning problems in later life.

Warning Signs That Interactions Are Inappropriate

It will not be difficult for you to determine if interactions are inappropriate. Observing in the classrooms, you will pick up on clues that indicate a need to provide guidance and support to teachers on establishing a more supportive climate. Here are some warning signs to look for and why they might be happening.

WARNING SIGNS	WHY THIS MIGHT BE HAPPENING
Teachers talk down to children or shout from across the room.	Teachers may not recognize the importance of eye contact and feel that a loud voice is more effective with young children.
Teachers constantly correct children and belittle them for forgetting the rules.	Teachers may lack the skills to guide children's behavior in positive ways.
Children are made to sit in a time-out chair when they have broken a rule or seem out of control.	Time-out is sometimes seen as an acceptable alternative to physical punishment but it can be emotionally abusive. Children rarely learn self-control from sitting in a time-out chair.
Teachers focus on misbehavior and fail to look for the causes.	It takes time to examine what might be causing a child's misbehavior and teachers may not have the skills or experience to do this.
Standards for behavior are not appropriate for children (e.g., high demands for sharing are placed on children, there are long waiting periods between activities, etc.).	Teachers may not understand normal child development and feel it is their role to get children to conform to adult standards.

Strategies for Working with Teachers on Positive Interactions

- Clarify the purpose of providing positive guidance and the importance of promoting social development.

- Participate in the classroom to model how you want teachers to interact with children.

- Post signs in the classrooms of the words you want teachers to use with the children. (e.g., "I can't let you hit because hitting hurts. I won't let anyone hit you either.")

- Show the videotape *The Creative Curriculum* and have teachers identify examples of positive interactions.

- Help teachers coping with a child's constant misbehavior to examine what might be causing the behavior and how they can work more effectively with the child.

Individualizing

Individualization is central to the *Creative Curriculum*. Although all children go through a consistent sequence in the development of skills and understandings, each child is a unique individual with special abilities, interests, and learning styles.

To assess whether the teachers understand how to individualize the program, you can begin by talking to them about the children in the classroom. The first step in individualizing the program is for teachers to learn as much as possible about each child. Ongoing observation of the children as they interact with materials and people and go through daily routines provides a lot of information on each child. Talking with parents about their children provides teachers with insights they might not gain while observing the children only in the center setting. Written documentation of the information in the form of anecdotal records, work samples, checklists, and summaries of conversations enables teachers to assess each child's progress and plan accordingly.

Obtaining information on each child is only the first step; teachers must know how to use the information to plan for each child's growth and development. Probably the most effective way to determine whether the staff is able to individualize is to visit the daily program. Reviewing the files on each child, observing the environment, and noting the interactions that take place between adults and children provide evidence of individualizing.

WHAT YOU SHOULD SEE	WHY
Teachers taking time to observe children during free play and to note insights they gain about each child's abilities, interests, and needs.	Careful observation of children in their natural environment is the best way to determine each child's real abilities and needs.
Asked about a particular child, teachers describe accurately the child's abilities and accomplishments, as well as goals and objectives for promoting the child's growth.	All teachers should recognize that each child is a unique individual with his/her own strengths, needs, and interests.
Children making choices regarding what activities they want to engage in and how to use the materials.	Self-selection enables children to participate in activities that are of interest to them.

Teachers responding to children in ways that demonstrate they know the children well and are taking into account their individual needs.

Daily interactions with each child provide excellent opportunities to meet individual needs.

Materials that reflect an understanding that children in the room are at different developmental levels and need to find materials that interest and challenge them.

One of the easiest ways to individualize is to offer children choices that are appropriate for their growing abilities and interests.

Teachers paying attention to children who are less verbal as well as to those who have a lot to say and who demand the attention of adults.

It is easy to ignore quiet children unless teachers have made a point to get to know each child.

Space, materials, and activities modified for children with handicapping conditions.

When children with handicapping conditions are mainstreamed, the environment should be adapted to enable each child to participate as fully as possible.

Teachers involved during most activity periods in interactions with one child or a small group of children.

It is easier to individualize the program when teachers are accustomed to working with children in small groups.

Warning Signs That Teachers Are Not Individualizing the Program

If teachers cannot describe each child's unique abilities and needs, observe the classroom for additional warning signs that the program is not individualized. Here are some signs to look for and possible explanations.

WARNING SIGNS

WHY THIS MIGHT BE HAPPENING

Teachers direct all activities according to a predetermined plan, whether or not the children seem interested and involved.

The focus is on what is to be taught and what the teachers want all children to learn rather than on the particular needs and interests of individual children in the group.

Standardized tests are the sole means used to determine each child's abilities and needs.

Teachers may feel they need to use standard measures to identify what children can and can't do as a basis for teaching them.

Teachers use the results of these tests to drill children so they can "do better."

Teachers may feel this is the best way to prepare children for school.

Activities are planned for the whole group rather than allowing children to select their own activities and work alone or in small groups.	When teachers plan a special activity, they sometimes want everyone to have a chance to participate.
Individual folders on each child contain no anecdotal records, observation notes, samples of the child's work, or notations from parent conferences.	Teachers may not have the skills they need to observe children and to document their observations.
The artwork displayed all looks the same.	Children are being given precut shapes and models to follow to produce "all-of-a-kind" artwork. Teachers may be expecting everyone to conform to adult standards.

Strategies for Working with Teachers on Individualizing

- Review children's individual files to see if they include several observations made by the staff, samples of children's work, notes from parent meetings, and objectives for learning.

- If individual files are inadequate or incomplete, give specific guidelines for what information should be in each folder and help teachers gather the data.

- Prepare observation notes on several children in the group and share them with the teachers as examples of how to document children's interactions with materials and people. Discuss what they have learned about each child and how they could use this information to individualize the program.

- Show the videotape *The Creative Curriculum* and have teachers observe the children who are featured. Discuss what they learned about the children and how the teachers met the individual needs of each child.

- Conduct regular meetings with teaching teams on individual children to discuss their observations of each child's abilities, interests, and needs. Help develop goals for each child and strategies for achieving these goals.

Parent Involvement

Basic to implementing the *Creative Curriculum* is a commitment to establishing a partnership with parents and to sharing information regularly about each child's progress. When parents are involved in the program in meaningful ways, everyone benefits. Parents feel they are part of a team and not abandoning their children during the day. The more parents learn about the program and the staff's goals for their children, the more they can extend and reinforce learning at home. Teachers benefit when parents share insights about their children and contribute to the program by donating their time and resources to enrich the curriculum. And children benefit the most when the significant adults in their lives are working together to give them the support and guidance they need to grow and develop. Trust is more easily established when children see that their two worlds are linked closely together.

In order to involve parents in the program in meaningful ways, all staff members must appreciate the importance of parent involvement and know how to achieve it. There are a number of strategies teachers can implement to promote meaningful parent involvement. Listed below are some examples of what you should expect to see and why these strategies are central to implementing the *Creative Curriculum*.

WHAT YOU SHOULD SEE	WHY
Teachers greeting parents by name when they bring children and pick them up.	Parents are a crucial part of the program their children attend, and they need to develop a sense of trust in the adults who care for their children.
Teachers sharing something about the child's day with each parent (e.g., a special interest, accomplishment, or anecdote).	Informal daily communication can be one of the best ways to keep parents informed about their child's life at school.
Teachers showing concern for parent's feelings when separation is difficult or the child has had a bad day.	Genuine concern for the parent's needs builds a strong bond between teachers and parents.
A parent bulletin board or message center at the entrance to each classroom, regularly updated and attractively displaying articles of interest to parents and announcements of important events.	A bulletin board or message center tells parents that they are important and the staff wants to keep them informed.
A parent corner filled with pamphlets and resources of interest to the parents and used for informal meetings.	Including a special place for parents conveys the message that their needs are considered important and they are always welcome.
Messages sent home weekly to share information on the program or about each child.	Weekly messages ensure that all parents receive the same information and that there is regular communication about each child.
Signs posted in each interest area conveying what children are learning and how parents can participate in extending their play.	When parents take time to volunteer in the classroom, everything should be done to ensure that the experience is successful and meaningful.
Parents encouraged to participate in the program by sharing a skill or interest or some aspect of their cultural heritage.	Parents have a lot to contribute to the program to enrich the curriculum.
Regularly scheduled parent meetings to discuss topics of interest to parents, to hear guest speakers, and to learn about the curriculum.	The more parents know about the program, the more they can support the efforts of the teaching staff to promote children's growth and development.

Parent/teacher conferences held to share information and progress on each child; documentation of the results in each child's folder.

Parent/teacher conferences are an excellent way to gain a total understanding of each child and how to best meet each child's needs.

Warning Signs That Parents Are Not Meaningfully Involved

Assessing the level of parent involvement requires more than a visit to the daily program. Some of the indicators are subtle and take time to uncover. If you note any of the warning signs listed below, you should be concerned about how effectively parents are being involved.

WARNING SIGNS	WHY THIS MIGHT BE HAPPENING
Teachers complain about the parents interfering in the program.	Teachers may not take the time to explain the program to parents and to respond to their concerns and wishes.
Parents view teachers as the experts and feel they have no role in the program.	Teachers may not feel comfortable explaining the program or defining a role for parents.
Parents drop off their children and quickly leave without staying to talk to the staff or observe the program.	Teachers may have conveyed the message that it is better for the children if the transition is brief.
No bulletin board has been set up with announcements for parents, or the one established is rarely changed or updated.	Teachers may not see this as part of their responsibility.
Parent meetings are poorly attended, and teachers blame the parents for lack of interest.	Teachers may need more support in designing parent meetings that are responsive to parent's interests, needs, and schedules.

Strategies for Working with Staff on Parent Involvement

- Meet with the teaching teams and the center director, if appropriate, to discuss your observations and to plan strategies for enhancing the involvement of parents in the program.

- Work with teachers to design a survey of parents on what issues they would like to have addressed at a parent meeting.

- At a staff meeting, help teachers identify the barriers that limit effective parent involvement and discuss ways to overcome these barriers.

- Share with teachers the ways in which parents might be involved using the suggestions in each module of the *Creative Curriculum*.

- Plan an open house when parents can visit the center and learn about the program through hands-on activities.

- Work with teachers to develop posters for each interest area explaining what children are learning and how to extend their learning. Invite parents to visit and participate in the program.

- Plan a workshop on how to conduct a parent conference, using role plays to practice suggested approaches.

Providing support to staff on implementing the *Creative Curriculum* is an ongoing responsibility. Classroom visits are one of the most effective ways to remain in touch with teachers' successes as well as the difficulties they are encountering.

This chapter concludes Part One of the *Guide*. Part Two provides specific workshops based on each of the modules in the *Creative Curriculum*.

Part Two

Workshops on the *Creative Curriculum*

Page

I.   **Workshop Strategies**... 55

     Planning for the Workshop.. 55

     Conducting the Workshop.. 56

     Follow-Up.. 57

II.   **Setting the Stage Workshops** 58

     How Children Think and Learn.. 59

     Promoting Children's Social Competence 74

     The Physical Environment 77

III. **Block Workshops** 84

     The Importance of Blocks 85

     Math Concepts and Problem Solving in Block Play......................... 92

     Blocks as a Medium for Dramatic Play.................................... 95

IV.   **House Corner Workshops** 97

     The Importance of Dramatic Play 98

     The Role of Props in Dramatic Play 101

     Follow-Up on Using Prop Boxes 106

     The Teacher's Role 111

V.   **Table Toy Workshops**...113

     The Importance of Table Toys 114

     Evaluating Table Toys...117

     The Teacher's Role..123

VI.   **Art Workshops** 125

   The Importance of Art.. 126

   Setting Up the Art Area: The Physical Environment................................. 130

   The Teacher's Role 133

VII.   **Sand and Water Workshops** 137

   Creating Learning Opportunities with Sand and Water............................. 138

   Exploring Math and Science Concepts with Sand and Water........................ 141

VIII.   **Library Workshops**... 145

   Reading to Young Children.. 146

   Selecting Books for Young Children.. 150

   Extending Literature through Creative Activities 153

IX.   **Music and Movement Workshops** 155

   The Importance of Music and Movement 156

   Making Music 164

   Movement Activities... 168

X.   **Cooking Workshops** 172

   The Importance of Cooking 173

   Learning Math and Science through Cooking 177

   Cooking to Go 181

XI.   **Computer Workshops**.. 185

   The Importance of Computers 186

   Critically Evaluating Software 190

   Mirroring other Activity Areas 193

XII.   **Outdoor Workshops**... 196

   The Importance of Outdoor Play.. 197

   Creating the Outdoor Environment 202

   The Teacher's Role 208

I. Workshop Strategies

Workshops are one of the most effective ways to convey the philosophy and approach of the *Creative Curriculum*. Although some teachers will pick up the curriculum, read it, and be able to implement it easily in their classrooms, other teachers may need more support to absorb the content and learn how to apply the suggested strategies.

This part of the *Guide* offers workshop outlines and handouts for conducting staff development sessions on the *Creative Curriculum*. As you read through these workshops, you will be able to identify those which are most appropriate for your program. Appropriateness will depend on what needs you are trying to address in your program, what workshop strategies you feel comfortable with, and the preferred learning styles of your staff. The workshops are designed for active learning, as this is the way most of us learn best.

Planning for the Workshop

Good planning and attention to details, including the physical environment, can help ensure the success of a workshop.

- **Attend to basic needs.** Trainers don't always have control over the setting for training, yet ensuring the physical comfort of participants can greatly enhance their ability to participate and learn. To the extent possible, ensure that there is comfortable, adult-size seating, adequate lighting, and appropriate temperature control in the workshop room. Provide food for participants and add decorative touches to make the table attractive such as a tablecloth and fresh flowers.

- **Prepare the agenda and handouts you will use.** Plan the agenda and handouts you will need and be sure you have enough copies for all participants. The agenda should give people a road map of what you will cover and when breaks are scheduled.

- **Review the content you will present.** Even if you have given the same workshops many times before, it's a good idea to review the content and exercises you plan to use ahead of time. Think of some new ways to present information, new stories you can share, insights you have gained since the last time you presented on the same topic. You will enjoy the workshop more if it's not the same old format and information you have shared in the past. Your enthusiasm will be contagious.

- **Organize the information in a useful way.** Provide whatever support you may need for yourself in order to feel comfortable in presenting the content: notes on index cards, highlighting information in the *Guide*.

- **Gather materials you will need for the workshop.** Review the list of materials needed for each workshop. If you plan to use audio-visual equipment, be sure it is in working order. It's always a good idea to bring or arrange for an extra bulb for the slide projector, an extension cord, and an adapter just in case they are needed.

- **Set up the room before participants arrive.** Whether participants will be sitting in a circle or at tables, arrange the room so that everyone can see you and, to the extent possible, all other participants. If you want participants to sit with people they don't know, plan a system for assigning them to tables randomly. For example, you might number each table and have participants select a number from a box telling them which table to sit at. (If you have four people at a table, you would need four pieces of paper for each number.)

Conducting the Workshop

The techniques you use in a staff development session and how you communicate with participants convey powerful messages. In many ways, your training style is as important as the information you present. You serve as a model for how you want participants to work with young children. When you conduct a workshop, consider the powerful messages implied in the following suggested techniques.

- **Create a social environment for learning.** Plan an exercise or ice-breaker to help people get to know one another and relax. If the group members are already acquainted, allow time for greetings and sharing before plunging into the content. Make sure everyone knows where to find the bathrooms, where they can smoke, and when lunch or snacks will be served.

- **Discuss the plans for the session.** Go over the agenda and the purpose of the workshop. Clarify when you plan to break and what time the workshop will end. Honor the commitments. Ask for questions or concerns that anyone may have.

- **Build the training on the experiences of participants.** Every workshop is unique because of the experiences and backgrounds of the participants. Encourage group members to share their knowledge of the topic, successful strategies for dealing with specific problems, and approaches to caring for young children.

- **Share your own experiences.** When you are open to sharing real experiences of your own, participants view you as a person with similar concerns. As a result, they are more likely to share openly their own experiences.

- **Be an active listener.** Before responding, rephrase what you thought was said to clarify a participant's question or statement. Check out whether you understood correctly.

- **Ask open-ended questions.** Asking questions that require recall, analysis, creative solutions, or evaluation provokes thought and problem solving. *What do you think about...? How would you handle that situation...?* and so on. Convey that you are not the only expert in the room by redirecting a question that a participant asks you to other participants to encourage them to share their views and experiences: *That's a tough problem. Does anyone have a suggestion on how to deal with the situation?*

- **Explain the exercises clearly.** Repeat instructions to make sure that all participants understand the directions. Move around the room to offer assistance to individuals or groups who are unclear about the task.

- **Encourage active participation but allow for individual differences.** By planning small group activities, you ensure that everyone can participate in a way that is comfortable for them. Some people enjoy doing role plays, reporting to the full group, or being videotaped; others are comfortable talking only in a small group. It is important to respect their feelings and provide a variety of ways for everyone to participate.

- **Handle conflict and disagreements without becoming defensive.** Participants may disagree with what you present or with the comments, suggestions, or opinions of their peers. Promote discussion of all viewpoints and acknowledge that there may be several ways of looking at the situation. Encourage participants to examine their own ideas and those of others based on their knowledge of child development.

- **Lead a final exercise in the training session.** Use this exercise to encourage staff to plan ways to implement what they have learned. Ask participants to think about and identify at least one way they will use what they have learned when they are working with children.

Follow-Up

Follow-up is important for two reasons: to determine whether the information and skills gained during a staff development session are actually used in the classroom, and to reinforce and support learning. Some suggested techniques to encourage staff to put new information and ideas into action, and to continue learning, appear below.

- **Provide an assignment to be completed over the next few weeks.** This should be something that staff can complete while working with children. The assignment might include a self-evaluation page that each individual completes and returns to you. You can review the self-evaluations to determine whether the training you have conducted is affecting staff performance.

- **Plan to spend time observing in participants' classrooms.** This will help you determine how they are applying their new knowledge and using new skills. Provide additional resources so that learning can continue.

- **Send out a post-training evaluation.** After several weeks have passed, disseminate a follow-up survey asking participants to give you feedback on the impact of the training. This information will be useful as you design future training sessions.

- **Plan a follow-up session on the same topic.** Use this time to discuss progress and experiences in applying what was learned.

The workshop strategies discussed in this chapter can be found in the workshops that follow.

II. Setting the Stage Workshops

In order to implement the *Creative Curriculum,* teachers must have an understanding of the philosophy that underlies its approach. One of the most effective ways to convey this philosophy is to conduct workshops that involve participants in activities designed to build an appreciation of the curriculum's child development focus.

The workshops outlined for setting the stage involve participants in firsthand research on children's thinking. One workshop addresses the importance of social competence and how teachers can promote children's social skills. Because the curriculum focuses on the environment, workshops are also recommended on this topic. This is a concrete place to begin helping teachers to implement the *Creative Curriculum* and one that ensures immediate and positive results in the classroom.

Workshops: **Page**

    How Children Think and Learn 59

    Promoting Children's Social Competence 74

    The Physical Environment.. 77

Handouts:

    "Anecdotes That Illustrate Young Children's Thinking" (Handout #1)............. 62

    "Animism Questionnaire" (Handout #2) 63

    "Animism Assignment" (Handout #3)... 68

    "Children's Drawings" (Handout #4) 71

    "Introduction to Room Arrangement" (Handout #5)................................. 80

    "Floor Plans" (Handout #6) 81

    "How the Environment Supports Socio-Emotional Development" (Handout #7).. 82

How Children Think and Learn

Participants in this workshop will:

- conduct firsthand research on how children think and view the world; and

- discuss the implications of this knowledge for planning the curriculum.

Materials needed:

- Index cards for each of the anecdotes (see Handout #1)

- Children's drawings of "what happens to the cookie after someone eats it"

- Chart paper and markers

- *The Creative Curriculum* videotape and VCR

Handouts:

- "Anecdotes That Illustrate Young Children's Thinking" (Handout #1)

- "Animism Questionnaire" (Handout #2)

- "Animism Assignment" (Handout #3)

Introducing the Topic:

- Explain that one of the enjoyable aspects of working with young children is that they have unique ways of explaining and learning about the world around them.

- Indicate that this workshop will involve participants in making their own discoveries about how young children think and learn.

- List on chart paper and discuss briefly the following principles about how young children think and learn:

  > Children have their own view of the world; they see and understand the world differently from adults. In order to understand children and help them love learning, adults must listen carefully, observe closely, and take children's ideas seriously.

  > Children learn through their play and by observing carefully what happens around them.

  > Children are more likely to remember connections they make themselves.

  > Development takes time; trying to hurry children through each stage does not benefit them.

Activity: How Children View the World

Ask participants to sit at one of three tables in the room. Each group will have a different set of materials to examine:

- Children's drawings of "what happens to the cookie after someone eats it"

- Anecdotes on index cards

- "Animism Questionnaire"

Explain that the purpose of this activity is to look at examples of children's drawings, sayings, and responses to a set of questions about what is alive and what is not alive. After reviewing the set of materials on the table, ask each group to respond to the following questions:

- "What can you learn about children's thinking?"

- "How does their thinking change over time?"

Allow 10 to 15 minutes for the groups to review each of the three sets of materials. Then lead a discussion to summarize their observations.

Cookie Pictures

In discussing participants' observations of how children responded to the task of drawing "what happens to the cookie after someone eats it" you will want to bring out the following points:

- Three- and four-year-old children draw the cookie itself or someone putting the cookie in his or her mouth. They are unable to think of something they have never seen (such as where the cookie goes after it is eaten).

- Five- to seven-year-olds understand that the cookie goes into their bodies and sometimes they draw the cookie in the stomach.

- Older children (eight to ten) have acquired a broader understanding of body parts and functions and can represent these concepts in great detail.

- Most children draw chocolate chip cookies.

Anecdotes

In discussing participants' observations of the anecdotes, try to elicit the following points about young children:

- They think in concrete terms.

- They focus on one attribute at a time (e.g., if a person is a policeman, he can't also be a daddy).

- They attribute human feelings and characteristics to inanimate objects.

- They think everyone knows what is on their mind.

- They judge things by how they look—if something looks like more, it is.

- They generalize from their experiences.

Animism Questionnaire

In discussing participants' observations of the "Animism Responses," emphasize the following points about young children:

- They believe that if something can move, it is alive.

- They often attribute human attributes to inanimate objects.

- If something is important to them (e.g., a pencil) or powerful (e.g., fire), they think it is alive.

- As children get older their information becomes more accurate, but sometimes they have a "cognitive conflict" (e.g., they think something is half alive).

- Children like to share information and knowledge they have acquired if they think an adult is really interested in their ideas.

Discussion and Videotape: Implications for the Curriculum

Lead a discussion of how adults can promote children's thinking and learning:

- "Based on what you learned about children's thinking, what role should adults play in promoting learning?"

- "What do we want most children to learn in early childhood?"

List the responses from the group. Then show the videotape *The Creative Curriculum.* Ask participants to note ways in which the teachers respond to children and promote thinking and learning.

Summarize the workshop by asking if anyone wants to add ideas to the list after seeing the videotape.

Assignment:

Encourage participants to conduct their own research on what children of different ages think is alive and not alive. Distribute copies of the "Animism Assignment" (Handout #3) and plan a follow-up session to discuss their observations.

Handout #1: Anecdotes That Illustrate Young Children's Thinking

A teacher was using a record during a music activity. She said to the children, "I want you to move to the music." The children got up and walked over to the record player.

"He can't be your daddy. He's a policeman and policemen shoot people and put them in jail."

A three-year-old became very frightened when told by her mother, "You're burning up with fever."

A four-year-old was walking around with a bag of potato chips that he was squeezing to break up the chips. His mother asked why he was smashing the potato chips. His answer: "To make more."

A teacher remarked to a three-year-old who was painting at the easel, "What a soft green color you made." The child put down her brush and felt the green area on her picture.

"Today we are having fish. I know because when the teacher comes late we eat fish."

A child of four, told he had sharp eyes, felt his eyes with his hands and said to his mother, "But they don't feel sharp."

A three-year-old noticed some unpopped corn in the bottom of a pan and said, "I guess that popcorn didn't want to pop."

A four-year-old asked her father why the marble was sliding down the board. He began to explain about things that roll and inclined planes but was interrupted by his daughter who asked, "But does the marble know you are down there waiting for it?"

"A tree is alive. Its branches swing in the wind and the leaves fall down."

A group of three-year-olds were discussing the difference between mittens and gloves. Finally one little girl announced with full authority, "Mittens are little. When they grow up, they will be gloves."

A young child with a bad tooth was asked if it hurt. He replied, "Yes, can't you feel it?"

"A bicycle is alive because I ride it and the wheels go around."

"You're a teacher, you can't be a mommy too!"

Two children were each given an equally large cookie. One child broke his into four pieces and announced, "Now I have more than you do."

Handout #2: Animism Questionnaire
(What's Alive and What's Not Alive)

Show the Child the Following Items	Tasanee (Three-and-a-half)	Natasha (Four)
Stone	*Yes, it's alive because it is hot.*	*Alive, because rocks are hard. If you throw rocks people get hurt.*
Pencil	*Yes, it's alive because it can write.*	*Alive, because pencils write.*
Broken Button	*No, because it's broken.*	*Alive, 'cause buttons are on dresses and sometimes on pants.*
Watch	*Yes, it's alive because it can turn.*	*Alive, because when it's time to go it's 8 o'clock.*
Chipped Dish	*No, it's not alive because it's a dish.*	*Alive, because sometimes little girls eat cereal in a bowl.*
Ask the Child about the Following Items		
Bicycle	*Yes! You can ride.*	*Alive, because so many people ride it and bikes are real!*
Chair	*Yes, it's alive because you can sit on it.*	*Alive, because people can sit in chairs and rocking chairs, too.*
Tree	*Yes, it's alive 'cause it can move its leaves, it is moving.*	*Alive, 'cause people shake trees, some trees sleep, and some wake up in the morning.*

Handout #2: Animism Questionnaire

Ask the Child about the Following Items	Tasanee (Three-and-a-half)	Natasha (Four)
Sun	*Yes, it's alive 'cause if you touch it it can burn you up and you can get dead.*	*Alive, because it will get hot, and sometimes it will get warm.*
Wind	*Yes, it's alive because it can blow, it moves.*	*Not alive, sometimes it gets cold and makes people cold and freezing.*
Car	*Car, yes it's alive, 'cause it can move.*	*Alive, cause some people can drive cars.*
Fire	*Yes, fire is alive because it can burn you up.*	*Alive, because it burns. Sometimes it burns people up and they put water on it and it makes smoke.*
Dog	*Yes, the dog is alive because it can move and run.*	*Alive, because my dog don't have no training. We have to put him in another school. He jumps and comes in the house and runs upstairs.*
Flower	*No, flowers are not alive. They can't walk.*	*Alive, because people pick flowers, wash them to make them clean and put them in a bowl. Then flowers grow.*
River	*Yes, because sh, sh, sh! it can move.*	*Alive, because people can swim in it.*
Clouds	*Yes, they go slow but look, look! they can move. (She was watching the sky)*	*Alive, because they are brown and white and shiny and bright and they move slow.*
Use this space to record any impressions you have or patterns you notice.		

Handout #2: Animism Questionnaire

Show the Child the Following Items	Lane (Six)	Ricky (Nine)
Stone	*Not alive. Not like the human being.*	*Not alive. Because it's just a rock. It does not have a heart, it doesn't have blood. It doesn't have cells. Rock comes from the earth, they don't feed on anything.*
Pencil	*Not alive.*	*Not alive. It has lead in it. If anything has lead in it it dies.*
Broken Button	*Not alive because it's for sewing.*	*Not alive. It's solid...nothing in it. It does not live. It does not grow.*
Watch	*Kind of...some work by batteries or electricity. Half alive.*	*Not alive. Because it does not have a heart or anything. It's a piece of machinery.*
Chipped Dish	*Not alive.*	*Not alive. If anything alive is chipped a millimeter or centimeter deep, the dirt will cause germs in your body and if it's not taken out, you have to have your arm cut off. When plates are chipped they don't have to have anything cut off.*
Bicycle	*Half alive, because it goes around. But it can't talk like a bird.*	*Not alive. A bicycle does not grow. Everything that is alive, grows. A bicycle has to be used and it must be controlled by man. Living things do not have to be used by man.*

Handout #2: Animism Questionnaire

Ask the Child about the Following Items	Lane (Six)	Ricky (Nine)
Chair	*Not alive, except a rocking chair. It's half...or one that goes around, but it doesn't talk.*	*Not alive. Because a chair is motionless and does not grow.*
Tree	*Yes, it's alive. Well, half because it's not a human being.*	*Alive. Because it grows and has a bark like human skin.*
Sun	*Half alive. Doesn't really move.*	*Not alive. Because it is a star and if anything is that hot it will burn like the sun.*
Wind	*Half alive. Not like us.*	*Not alive. A wind is caused when warm air goes under cold air at the equator.*
Car	*Half alive when it's running on gas.*	*Not alive. It's a piece of machinery and does not grow.*
Fire	*Half alive, the flames can kill someone.*	*Not alive. Because it is when wood burns and wood is usually dead when you put it in the fire.*
Dog	*Alive because it barks, eats, sleeps and lives.*	*Alive. Because it grows.*
Flower	*Half alive. I don't know why.*	*Alive. Because it starts with a little seedling and grows into a nice pretty flower.*
River	*Half alive, fish and waterfalls and boats make it move.*	*Not alive. Because water comes from a spring and it flows into a river. But it does grow.*

Handout #2: Animism Questionnaire

Ask the Child about the Following Items	Lane (Six)	Ricky (Nine)
Clouds	*Half alive.*	*Not alive. Because clouds are only mist made of water that steams up from the ground.*
Use this space to record any impressions you have or patterns you notice.		

Handout #3: Animism Assignment

Purpose:

The purpose of this assignment is to gain a better understanding of how children think at different stages of development. When adults ask children questions and listen respectfully to their responses, children are more likely to share their ideas openly. By recording exactly what a child says and then reviewing the child's responses to all the questions, we can begin to see patterns in their thinking that help us understand how this young child views the world. Posing the same questions to children at different ages can give us insights into how children's thinking changes as they grow.

Instructions:

Conduct interviews with several children whose ages may vary from 3 to 10 years. Take time to talk with each child individually and record exactly what the child says on the attached chart.

You might introduce the topic in the following way: "I have some questions I want to ask you because I'm interested in what you think. I'm going to write down exactly what you say to help me remember. Do you know what it means to be alive? Are you alive? Is a cat alive? How do you know?"

Begin by showing the child the first five objects on the list, one at a time. Say: "Is this stone alive?" "How do you know it is (or is not) alive?"

It's important not only to find out what the child thinks is alive or not alive but also to understand the reason behind the response.

If you wish, tape record the session so you can be sure to capture each word. Later, you can fill out the chart.

Animism Questions

NAME AND AGE OF CHILD

Show the Child the Following Items		
Stone		
Pencil		
Broken Button		
Watch		
Chipped Dish		
Ask the Child about the Following Items		
Bicycle		
Chair		
Tree		

Ask the Child about the Following Items		
Sun		
Wind		
Car		
Fire		
Dog		
Flower		
River		
Clouds		
Use this space to record any impressions you have or patterns you notice.		

Handout #4: Children's Drawings
"What Happens to the Cookie after Someone Eats It"

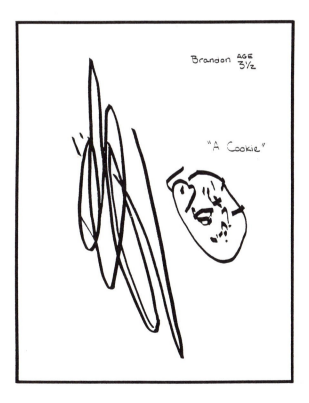

Koren AGE 5

tummy

leg Body leg

Cookie inside

Grandma ate a cookie. She has eaten it & now it is in her tummy.

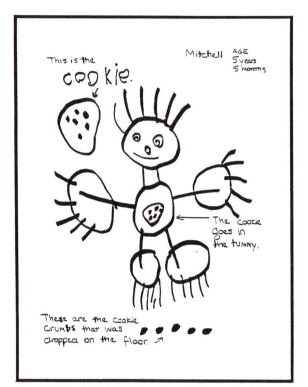

Mitchell AGE 5 years 5 months

This is the cookie.

The cookie goes in the tummy.

These are the cookie Crumbs that was dropped on the floor.

I like to eat cookies. I like to snitch cookies. I take the cookie & I eat it & then it goes into my tummy.

David AGE 7

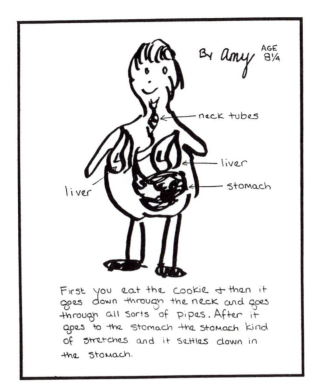

By amy AGE 8¼

neck tubes

liver

liver

stomach

First you eat the cookie & then it goes down through the neck and goes through all sorts of pipes. After it goes to the stomach the stomach kind of stretches and it settles down in the stomach.

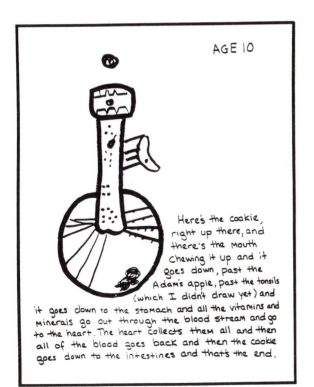

AGE 10

Here's the cookie, right up there, and there's the mouth chewing it up and it goes down, past the Adam's apple, past the tonsils (which I didn't draw yet) and it goes down to the stomach and all the vitamins and minerals go out through the blood stream and go to the heart. The heart collects them all and then all of the blood goes back and then the cookie goes down to the intestines and that's the end.

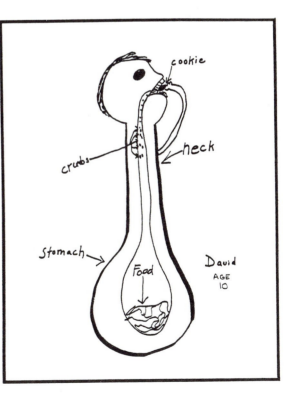

cookie

neck

crubs

Stomach

Food

David
AGE
10

Promoting Children's Social Competence

Participants in this workshop will:

- develop a definition of social competence;

- identify the reasons children might lack social competence;

- learn about the research findings on the importance of social competence; and

- identify ways to promote children's social skills.

Materials needed:

- Chart pad and markers

- VCR and TV monitor

- Videotape: *The Creative Curriculum*

Discussion: Defining Social Competence

Ask participants to think of a child in their classroom who has developed social competence. What behaviors and attitudes does this child exhibit?

You may hear ideas such as the following expressed.

- a strong sense of self-esteem
- enthusiastic about coming to school
- able to separate from parents without great difficulty
- asks and answers questions
- curious and eager to explore
- willing to take risks
- uses materials well and treats them with respect
- cooperative and cheerful
- well-developed language skills
- able to enter a group and be accepted
- demonstrates empathy and concern for others
- able to sustain play and complete tasks

After generating this list, ask participants to think of a child in their class who has very poor social skills, who is has difficulty making a friend, entering a group, or relating positively to others. It might help to have people close their eyes and remember some recent behaviors and episodes with this child. Then invite each person to share one characteristic of the child in their class who lacks social competence.

You may generate a list similar to the one below.

- aggressive in play and when relating to others
- withdrawn and fearful of other children
- cursory involvement with materials
- unable to enter a group of children and be accepted
- poor language skills
- constantly needs direction from the teacher
- clinging behavior and constant need for adult attention
- falls apart when there are changes in the routines
- unable to play for a sustained time or be creative
- fixated on the media and on violence
- regressive behavior such as thumb-sucking and ticks

Generating these two lists leads easily into a discussion of why teachers are seeing more and more children today who lack social competence. Teachers across the country talk about the increasing number of children who are experiencing a great deal of stress in their lives and come to school with serious emotional problems.

Pose the question: "What might be some reasons why so many children are failing to develop social competence today?" Your discussion could focus on the following factors:

- They live in unstable family situations where poverty, violence, and abuse are commonplace. If they don't experience violence at home, they see it on television and in their neighborhoods.

- They haven't been taught how to approach other children in ways that are likely to be successful and so they are aggressive and bossy in their interactions. The rejection they experience leads them to push harder and this only exacerbates the situation.

- They are not able to verbalize their feelings and wishes in order to communicate effectively with peers and adults. Therefore, other children have difficulty knowing what they need or want.

- They have not developed self-control and therefore do not know how to wait for a turn, how to negotiate with others, and how to resolve conflicts successfully without resorting to aggression.

- The curriculum is not developmentally appropriate and children are expected to know how to sit quietly, listen to and follow verbal directions, and complete worksheets on concepts they have not experienced firsthand. Because they are bored and frustrated, they act out and disturb others, getting themselves constantly in trouble.

Conclude this discussion by sharing the research findings that confirm the importance of helping children develop social skills. An excellent resource is *The Teacher's Role in the Social Development of Young Children* by Lilian G. Katz and Diane E. McClellan (ERIC Clearinghouse on Elementary and Early Childhood Education, Urbana, IL, 1991). Research findings summarized in this document (p. 1) include the following:

- Cognitive development cannot be separated from social development. Children learn in the context of their social relationships as they observe and interact with peers and adults.

- Children who achieve social competence by the time they are in kindergarten are more likely to succeed academically and socially in later grades.

- Children who do not achieve social competence in their relationships with peers are at risk of developing serious problems in later childhood and as adults. This includes dropping out of school, juvenile delinquency, and an inability to maintain meaningful relationships.

Refer participants to the checklist at the back of the *Creative Curriculum* and review the behaviors listed under Socio-Emotional Development.

Videotape: *The Creative Curriculum*

In the videotape on *The Creative Curriculum,* there are many examples of how children are developing social skills and self-confidence. When you show the videotape, ask participants to note how children are acquiring social skills and how teachers support children's self-esteem and ability to get along with others. Note particularly scenes in the block section where two children try to exclude a child from building; the teacher who understood a child's need for attention in the library area; and the group scene at the end with the ducks.

Activity: How Teachers Can Promote Social Competence

There are many ways in which teachers promote social competence. In this activity, divide the group into several teams and give each a large chart of paper and set of markers. Each team will discuss and develop a list of ideas for helping children develop social skills in the following categories:

- How teachers can use group meetings to help children feel part of the group and develop social skills.

- How teachers can serve as models and mentors to help children develop social skills.

- How the daily schedule and routines can help children develop social skills.

Refer participants to the relevant sections in the *Creative Curriculum* for additional ideas.

Follow-up Activity: Assessing a Child's Social Competence

Encourage teachers to use the Checklist in the *Creative Curriculum* to assess children's socio-emotional development. This information on each child's development can be very helpful in designing ways to intervene and help children who need support in developing social competence.

The Physical Environment

Participants in this workshop will:

- learn how behavior is affected by the physical environment;

- discuss the advantages and disadvantages of two floor plans of the same classroom;

- view a filmstrip on how room arrangement can affect children's behavior; and

- identify ways to organize the classroom to support socio-emotional and cognitive development.

Materials needed:

- VCR and TV monitor

- Slide/Videotape: *The New Room Arrangement as a Teaching Strategy*

- Chart pad and markers

- Poster board, markers, construction paper, clear contact paper, and scissors

Handouts:

- "Introduction to Room Arrangement" (Handout #5)

- "Floor Plans" (Handout #6)

- "How the Environment Supports Socio-Emotional Development" (Handout #7)

Activity: How the Environment Affects Behavior

As participants enter the workshop, distribute Handout #5: "Introduction to Room Arrangement." While they wait for the workshop to start, ask them to respond to the questions.

Lead a discussion on how we are all affected by our environment using the questions in the handout. Note participants' responses on chart paper. You may hear ideas such as the following expressed.

- A store I dislike shopping in:

  unattractive displays
  cluttered and disorganized
  difficult to find what I want
  long waits
  narrow aisles
  dark and dingy
  no logical order to displays

poor selection
noisy
unhelpful sales people
loud music

- A store I like to shop in:

  attractive and inviting displays
  clean and well kept
  soft music
  well organized
  helpful sales people
  soft carpeting
  well lit
  well-organized check-outs

- Behavior I want to encourage:

  independence
  curiosity
  appropriate use of materials
  consideration of others
  cooperation and sharing
  enthusiasm and excitement
  involvement and the ability to stick with a task
  joyfulness
  respect for materials
  respect for the feelings and needs of others
  willingness to take risks and try out ideas

- Behavior I want to discourage:

  running around the room
  resistance to clean-up
  inability to make choices—wandering behavior
  inability to stick with a task
  fighting over toys

Conclude the activity by noting that like children, adults are also affected by their environment. Explain that a well-organized and rich environment can address many of the behavior problems that participants identified.

Activity: Floor Plans

Distribute Handout #6: "Floor Plans." Ask participants to look at the two arrangements of the same room and note the advantages and disadvantages of each one. Participants can do this individually or with a partner.

Lead a discussion asking participants to share their observations. For Plan A, the following views may be expressed:

- Too much open space will encourage running.

- The block area is too open—block structures will be kicked over easily.

- The library area shouldn't be near a noisy area such as blocks.

- Areas are not clearly defined.

For Plan B you may hear the following:

- Areas are clearly defined by shelves.
- The block corner near the house corner will encourage dramatic play.
- The block builders are more protected.
- Quiet areas are separated from noisy activity areas.
- The house corner has two distinct rooms—it's more like a real home.
- Children will be more protected from distractions in other areas.

Ask participants to use the back of the handout to draw a floor plan of their own room and to list what changes they want to make.

Slide/Videotape: *The New Room Arrangement as a Teaching Strategy*

Distribute Handout #7: "How the Environment Supports Socio-Emotional Development." Review the first three stages of life as defined by Erik Erikson. Ask participants to list some of the ways that the environment can be organized to support the development of trust, autonomy and initiative.

Introduce the slide/videotape by explaining that room arrangement and the way materials are displayed in an early childhood classroom are powerful teaching strategies that can support teacher's goals for children.

Identify the four principal goals that are addressed in the videotape:

- to help children learn to trust their environment and get along with others;

- to develop independence: the ability to make choices and be responsible about cleaning up and putting materials away where they belong;

- to be able to focus on an activity and become involved in their work; and

- to acquire new skills and concepts.

Invite participants to view the presentation with these goals in mind and to add to their list other ways that the environment can support their goals.

After showing the slide/videotape, discuss the four major strategies for organizing an effective learning environment:

- clearly defined activity areas;
- well-established routines;
- attractive and logical display of materials; and
- the creativity to continuously adapt and enhance the environment.

Note that each of the modules in the *Creative Curriculum* suggests ways to organize and continually enrich each interest area.

Handout #5: Introduction to Room Arrangement

As part of this workshop, take a few minutes to jot down your responses to these questions:

1. Think of a store where you **dislike** shopping. What makes it frustrating and unpleasant to shop in this store?

2. Think of a store where you **like** to shop. What makes it easy and pleasant to shop in this store?

3. How many of the characteristics you listed above also apply to the classroom environment?

Handout #6: Floor Plans

Advantages/Disadvantages

Plan A

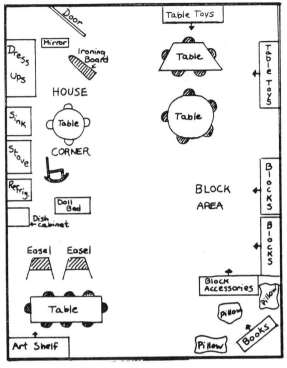
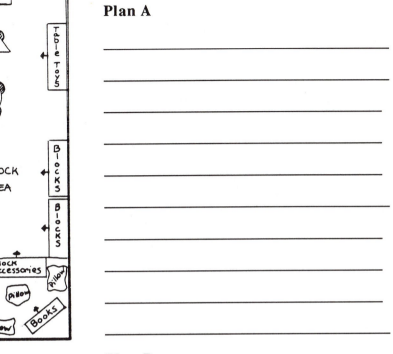

_____

_____

_____

_____

_____

_____

_____

_____

_____

_____

Plan B

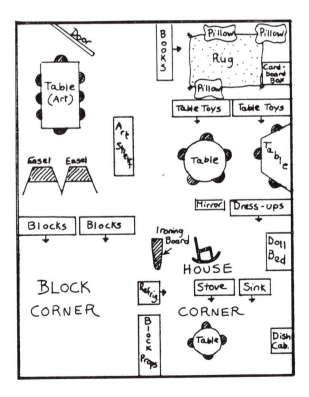

_____

_____

_____

_____

_____

_____

_____

_____

_____

_____

_____

Handout #7: How the Environment Supports Socio-Emotional Development

Erik Erikson described the eight stages of socio-emotional growth, from infancy to old age. At each stage, we confront certain socio-emotional issues. How these issues are handled impacts on our character and development. According to Erikson, during the first stage of development, infants learn to either trust or mistrust their environment. If they are fed when they are hungry, changed when they are soiled, and comforted when they are upset, infants learn that the world is a place they can trust. This sense of trust gives them the security to venture out and explore the world. During the second stage of life, toddlers are learning about self-control and independence. If adults are accepting and encourage their emerging sense of self, toddlers develop autonomy. During the preschool years, children are interested in exploring, creating, and expressing their natural sense of curiosity. Adults can help children resolve these important issues successfully, or they can hamper their development as illustrated in the chart below.

The issues that children are dealing with during the first three stages identified by Erikson are summarized in the chart below.

Trust	Mistrust
I can depend on you to meet my needs.	I can't depend on you.
This is a safe place.	I'm not safe here.
Autonomy	**Shame and Doubt**
I can do it myself.	I probably can't do it.
You approve of me.	You don't approve of me.
Initiative	**Guilt**
I want to try to figure things out.	I'm doing it wrong.
I can take risks and make mistakes.	I'd better not try.

The physical environment of the classroom can support the development of trust, autonomy and initiative. In the blank chart on the next page, identify some of the ways the environment can convey the messages we want children to receive.

	Messages We Want to Convey to Children	How the Physical Environment Can Convey These Messages
Trust	*I can depend on you to meet my needs.* *This is a safe place.*	
Autonomy	*I can do it myself.* *You approve of me.*	
Initiative	*I want to try to figure things out.* *I can take risks and make mistakes.*	

III. Block Workshops

Participating in block workshops gives teachers an opportunity to discover for themselves the many values of block play in the classroom. As they work with unit blocks, props, and accessories, teachers observe firsthand the numerous math and science concepts that children discover through block play. They also recognize how blocks promote dramatic play, creativity, and imagination.

When teachers understand the importance and versatility of blocks, they are better able to support children's play in the block corner. They appreciate even more the satisfaction and enjoyment children experience when they use blocks to give concrete form to their ideas and feelings.

Workshops: **Page**

    The Importance of Blocks.. 85

    Math Concepts and Problem Solving in Block Play 92

    Blocks as a Medium for Dramatic Play 95

Handouts:

    "Developmental Stages of Block Play" 88

The Importance of Blocks

Participants in this workshop will:

- identify the value of blocks in the classroom;

- learn the stages of development in children's block play;

- give examples of how playing with blocks enhances growth and development; and

- identify common concerns teachers have about using blocks.

Materials needed:

- Wooden unit blocks with all shapes included; enough blocks for at least half of the participants to build with at the same time

- Chart pad, markers, and tape

Handout:

- "Developmental Stages of Block Play" (Handout #1)

Activity: Exploring with Blocks

Invite participants to select some blocks and find a space on the floor. Explain that you will be playing the role of the teacher. Give the following directions:

> "In this activity, you will have a chance to build with blocks You don't have to make anything in particular, just look at the block shapes and let your structure develop as you build."

During this activity, move through the room and record on paper anything the participants say that relates to concepts children discover through blocks for example, "this is too long," "I need that one," "it's too high," "it won't fit," and so on. You can use these examples later on to illustrate the concepts that children can learn when playing with blocks.

When participants have finished building, distribute copies of the handout "Developmental Stages of Block Play." Ask participants to look at their own structures to find examples of the different stages observed when children build with blocks—piling, enclosing, bridging, designing, and making elaborate structures.

Discussion: Why Block Play Is Valuable

Lead a discussion on the values of block play by asking questions such as the following:

- "What did you enjoy most about using the blocks?"

- "Did you have any problems finding the blocks you needed?"

Note the responses on the chart pad. In summarizing the discussion, include points such as the following:

- Children can put their ideas into concrete form with blocks.

- Children enjoy the sense of mastery and control that block play provides.

- Blocks stimulate creativity and imagination; there are no "right" or "wrong" ways to build with blocks.

Small Group Exercise: What Children Learn Through Block Play

Explain that block play enhances growth and development in all areas: social, emotional, physical, and cognitive. Divide the group into four teams and ask each team to think of examples of how block play enhances growth in each developmental area. Ask them to base their comments on what they did with the blocks themselves, what they observed their partner doing, and what they have seen children do with blocks in the classroom. If the group has seen the videotape on the *Creative Curriculum*, ask them to recall the various scenes in the block area. Allow approximately 10 minutes for the activity. Then list each group's responses on a chart.

Social Development	Emotional Development	Physical Development	Cognitive Development

Add your own comments, based on what you observed as the participants used blocks (e.g., Martha asked Peter to lend her the circle; when Joan ran out of quadruple units, she replaced them with two double-unit blocks).

Examples of what participants may list for each developmental area appear below. (See the module on Blocks in the *Creative Curriculum* for additional goals and objectives for children in the block corner.)

Social

- Learn to share, compromise, negotiate, and cooperate.

- Plan in small groups what and how to build.

Emotional

- Derive satisfaction from giving concrete form to their ideas.

- Express their feelings and show creatively how they view their world.

Physical

- Develop and refine small muscle skills and eye-hand coordination.

- Experience the physical properties of blocks as they pick them up, balance them, and so on.

Cognitive

- Talk about their constructions, which enhances language development.

- Observe firsthand many math, science, and physical concepts.

- Classify and sort sizes and shapes.

- Solve construction problems.

Discussion: Common Problems in the Block Corner

Teachers sometimes encounter problems using blocks in the classroom. Now that the values of block play have been identified, give participants an opportunity to express any concerns about blocks. Begin by asking:

"What are some of the problems you or the children have in using blocks effectively?"

Record the ideas on the chart pad. You might hear:

- blocks are noisy;
- there isn't enough room;
- the boys dominate the block corner;
- clean-up is difficult;
- the children have trouble sharing blocks and props; or
- the children knock into each other's buildings.

Note that many of the problems teachers encounter in the block corner can be alleviated through room arrangement, proper display of blocks and props, and supportive teacher/child interactions. Refer participants to the section on room arrangement in the module on Blocks in the *Creative Curriculum* for further ideas.

Handout #1: Developmental Stages of Block Play

As with all areas of development, children go through stages using blocks and they progress through these stages at different rates. Understanding the stages helps you gain realistic expectations of what children should be accomplishing as they play. For example, it is appropriate for a child first using blocks to carry the blocks around, and it is appropriate for an experienced five-year-old block builder to construct an intricate tower. Each child is exhibiting behaviors appropriate to his or her stage of development.

There are four stages in block use, each of which is briefly summarized below.

Stage I: Carrying Blocks (Functional Play)

Young children who haven't played with blocks before will carry them around or pile them in a truck and transport them. At this point, children are interested in learning about blocks—how heavy they are, what they feel like, and how many can be carried at once. By experimenting with blocks, children begin to learn their properties and gain an understanding of what they can and cannot do with blocks.

Stage II: Piling Blocks and Laying Blocks on the Floor

Piling blocks or organizing them on the floor is another stage of exploration. Children in Stage II continue to learn about the characteristics of blocks. They discover how to make a tower by piling blocks on top of each other and what different arrangements look like as they lie on the floor.

At this stage children also begin to apply imagination and critical thinking skills. To young builders, flat rows of blocks on the floor typically suggest a road. Props such as cars and trucks are frequently put to use if they are available to the block builders.

Stage III: Connecting Blocks to Create Structures (Constructive Play)

The use of roads during Stage II marks the transition from piling blocks to making actual constructions. Children who have become comfortable with road building find that they can use roads to link towers. This discovery leads to an active stage of experimentation as children apply their problem-solving skills.

Typically, children in Stage III (three- or four-year-olds) have had some experience with blocks. This experience enables them to approach blocks in new, creative ways. Typical among the construction techniques developed by children in Stage III are the following:

Making enclosures. Children put blocks together to enclose a space. At first, simply making the enclosure is a satisfying experience. Later, the enclosure may be used for dramatic play with zoo or farm animals. Enclosures help children think about mathematical concepts, particularly area and geometry.

Bridging. To make a bridge, children set up two blocks, leave a space between them, and connect the two blocks with another block. As with enclosures, children use bridges first as a construction technique and later as a mechanism for dramatic play enhancement. Bridging also teaches children balance and improves eye-hand coordination.

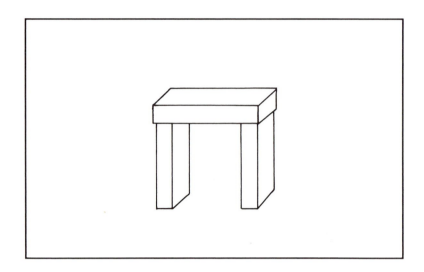

Designing. Children are fascinated with symmetry, balance, and patterns and begin to use blocks to form decorative patterns and symmetrical layouts. Once they have combined a few blocks in a certain way, they may continue the same pattern until their supply of blocks runs out. As they express themselves aesthetically, they notice similarities and differences and develop motor skills.

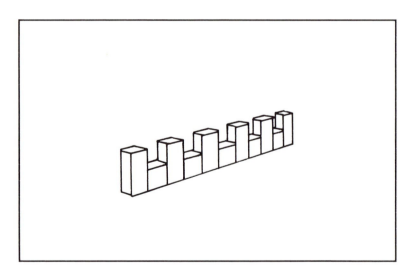

Stage IV: Making Elaborate Constructions (Dramatic Play)

Experienced builders (four- to six-year-olds) are able to put blocks together with dexterity and skill. Children learn to adapt to changes in their building area by curving structures and by building them above, around, or over obstacles. Children in Stage IV are adept in creating structures of remarkable complexity and ingenuity.

During this stage of development, children need a variety of block sizes and shapes so that they can make their constructions more elaborate. Another hallmark of Stage IV is that children are able to label their constructions. These labeled structures are often used as the setting for dramatic play.

Keep these stages in mind when you observe the children in your classroom. You will probably see evidence of all four stages.

Math Concepts and Problem Solving in Block Play

> **Participants in this workshop will:**
>
> • observe firsthand the many math concepts inherent in block play; and
>
> • use unit blocks to discover the kinds of problems that children create and solve with unit blocks.

Setting:

Whenever possible, this workshop should be conducted in a classroom setting where blocks and props are displayed and shelves are labeled as recommended in the *Creative Curriculum.*

Materials needed:

- Unit blocks on labeled shelves

- A large cardboard box

- Chart pad and markers

- *The Creative Curriculum* videotape and VCR

Activity: Discovering Mathematics through Block Play

Demonstrate for participants that unit blocks are so named because they are scaled to a unit size: two squares equal one unit, two units equal one double unit, and so on. Point out that there are other mathematical relationships that children discover which are less obvious. Ask participants to find a partner and work on one of the following tasks:

- "How many ways can you find to show math concepts or relationships with blocks (for example, four units equal one quadruple unit)?"

- "How many ways can you find to make geometric shapes with unit blocks?"

Allow approximately 5 to 10 minutes. Invite each team to share their discoveries with the rest of the group. Note all responses on the chart pad and add any that you observed.

In summarizing the experience, be sure to make the following points:

- Children discover many concepts through block play, including spatial relations, measurement and size, volume, and weight.

- Teachers can extend children's experiences by helping them identify and name the many concepts they discover. For example:

    What blocks are used: "You found out that two of these blocks make one long block."

Where the blocks were placed: "You used four blocks to make a big square."

How many blocks were used: "You used all the blocks to make the road."

(Refer participants to the *Creative Curriculum* for additional ideas on learning through block play.)

Now ask the group to put all the blocks away by requesting half the participants to put blocks on the labeled shelves and the other half to put blocks in the large cardboard box. Then ask each group to identify the advantages and disadvantages of each type of storage.

The group using the box for storage might note the following:

- "It was faster putting the blocks away in a box."

- "It was very noisy."

- "When blocks are in a box, you can't find what you need."

The group placing blocks on the labeled shelves might make the following observations:

- "It gave me a sense of satisfaction to see them put away in the correct place."

- "It took longer."

- "Putting the blocks on the shelf was fun—matching shapes made it into a game."

- "I was matching shapes with a label."

Activity: Solving Problems through Block Play

Explain that children create and then solve many problems for themselves through block play. They learn to negotiate, compromise, and cooperate. They also solve problems that relate to math, physics, and structure. To give participants firsthand experience in what young children do, assign each team one of the following tasks:

1. Build a ramp leading to a bridge.

2. Find a way to make five steps leading to a building.

3. Create a house with windows and a roof.

4. Build an apartment house with an elevator.

5. Make a "map" of your classroom or neighborhood using blocks.

Allow approximately 10 to 15 minutes. Write down anything participants say that illustrates a specific concept or skill that children develop through block play. Since this exercise is a cooperative one, pay close attention to examples of social skills and language development that you observe.

As you rotate among the groups, model the teacher's role by asking questions or commenting on your observations.

When the group has completed the tasks, lead a discussion of the problems they encountered and how they solved them. You might begin with questions such as these:

- "How did you solve the problems you were assigned?"

- "Was it more complicated than you thought?"

- "How do you think a child would have approached the same problem?"

As a follow-up, suggest that participants observe the children in their class and record examples of problem solving in block play.

Videotape: *The Creative Curriculum*

To conclude the workshop, show the portion of the videotape on blocks. Explain that there are two episodes in this portion that show teachers helping children to solve problems in the block area.

- A child learns how to make tall blocks stand up.

- A group of children learns how to cooperate in the block area.

Blocks as a Medium for Dramatic Play

Participants in this workshop will:

- see firsthand that blocks can be a setting for dramatic play;

- work cooperatively to create a dramatic play setting or theme; and

- discover how to enhance and encourage dramatic play in the block corner.

Materials needed:

- Unit blocks

- Basic props, including people, animals, and transportation vehicles (use labeled shelves if possible to illustrate the recommended display of props and accessories)

- Props such as colored cube blocks, string, spools, and rug scraps (see the module on Blocks for additional ideas)

- Chart pad and markers

Activity: Creating a Dramatic Play Theme with Blocks

Introduce the workshop by asking participants to name dramatic play themes that they have seen children create in the classroom. Record them on the chart pad. Explain that in this building experience, participants will be using props and accessories in addition to unit blocks.

Form groups of three or four and ask each group to decide on a theme they want to explore. Then give the following instructions:

- "Find a space on the floor that will be large enough and plan your construction."

- "You can use any props you see available. If you don't see what you need, use the scrap materials to create your own."

As the trainer, your job will be to model the role of the teacher in a classroom. This may involve a variety of teaching strategies.

- Observing what participants are doing:

    "I see you are making a farm."

- Asking questions to extend their ideas:

    "What do the animals on your farm eat?" "What will happen to the milk that the farmer has just taken from the cows?"

- Leading discussions:

  "Your farm has a house for the people and a barn for the animals. What else does your farm have?"

- Providing props or suggesting ways to make props to further stimulate play:

  "The fire engine you are using seems to need some more equipment. Let's see what we have on the table to make the things you need."

- Commenting on how their structures change as they expand their ideas.

  "You started with just a fire station and now you have a whole city."

After the groups have completed their buildings, spend a few minutes at each building site with the entire group to allow the builders to talk about their constructions: what they made; how it evolved; how it works. Sometimes participants will actually stage a dramatization on their theme. You might then ask questions such as the following:

- "How does this experience compare to what you've observed in the classroom?"

- "In what ways would it differ?"

- "How did using props make a difference?"

Participants may come up with some of the following points:

- Children's buildings would probably be much less elaborate.

- You would want to give children fewer props and supplies.

- Children wouldn't just build; they would use the scenes to act out roles; they'd want to *be* the policeman or *go* to the zoo.

To summarize the session, ask what participants noticed about the role you played as the teacher.

- "What did I as the teacher do to help you develop your block constructions?"

- "Was this helpful? How?"

- "Did you resent any of my suggestions as intrusions? Do children sometimes feel the teacher interferes too much?"

- "What can you do in your classroom to help dramatic play get started in the block corner?"

Discussion: Enhancing and Extending Children's Block Play

While the participants' structures are still up, lead a discussion on ways to preserve and extend children's efforts in the block corner. Refer to the section in the module on Blocks for a discussion on sign writing, taking pictures of block structures, leaving structures up for a few days, and other suggestions.

End the workshop by asking each participant to select one new thing he or she learned during the workshop to try in the classroom.

IV. House Corner Workshops

Most teachers and parents of young children recognize the natural appeal and popularity of the house corner. The primary purpose for offering workshops on the topic of dramatic lay is to demonstrate how children's play in the house corner enhances all areas of development. Through role playing and discussion, participants can gain skills in observing children's level of play. These observations can form the basis for designing strategies to extend children's play in the house corner.

Another reason for conducting workshops on the house corner is to provide teachers and parents with new ways of stimulating play by adding props and by transforming the house corner to represent new themes. In some classrooms the house corner remains unchanged throughout the year. In the *Creative Curriculum* the house corner evolves and provides new and challenging dramatic play scenes for children.

Workshops: **Page**

    The Importance of Dramatic Play.. 98

    The Role of Props in Dramatic Play... 101

    Follow-Up on Using Prop Boxes.. 106

    The Teacher's Role.. 111

Handouts:

    "Observing Dramatic Play" (Handout #1)... 100

    "Role Play Cards" (Handout #2)... 104

    "Using Prop Boxes in the House Corner" (Handout #3)........................... 105

    "Levels of Ability in Dramatic Play" (Handout #4) 107

Allow at least one week between sessions with assigned observations so that participants have time to complete the assignment.

The Importance of Dramatic Play

Participants in this workshop will:

- identify ways that dramatic play enhances social, emotional, physical, and intellectual development;

- describe what they like most about the house corner; and

- identify common concerns about the house corner.

Materials needed:

- Chart pad, markers, and tape

Handout:

- "Observing Dramatic Play" (Handout #1)

Discussion: The Value of Dramatic Play

Begin the session by explaining that dramatic play in the house corner offers many opportunities for children to develop social, emotional, physical, and cognitive skills. Divide the group into four teams. Assign each team one area of development: social, emotional, physical, and cognitive. Have participants identify all the ways in which dramatic play can enhance development in their area.

Allow approximately 10 to 15 minutes, then ask each team to report on their discussion. Record the ideas on a chart pad where you have listed the four developmental areas.

Social Development	Emotional Development	Physical Development	Cognitive Development

The following examples may be offered.

Social Development

- Replay different adult and family roles to better understand them.

- Interact with peers and learn to share, compromise, negotiate, and plan.

Emotional Development

- Express their feelings and perceptions of the world around them.

- Work through their feelings about events that have frightened and/or confused them (e.g., hospitalization, divorce, the birth of a sibling).

- Gain mastery of their feelings when they re-enact traumatic experiences and come to understand them.

Physical Development

- Enhance small muscle skills development by putting on dress-up clothes.

- Practice eye-hand coordination by matching props with labels, dressing dolls.

Cognitive Development

- Try out new ideas, create and solve many problems, and develop and refine their thinking skills.

- Practice language skills in the house corner.

(Refer participants to the House Corner module for additional ideas.)

Assignment:

End the session by explaining that it is often helpful to do a focused observation of children at play to really understand how much children are learning. Distribute Handout #1, "Observing Dramatic Play," and review the form. Ask participants to note examples of what children do in the house corner and how it contributes to their development in all areas.

Plan a time at a follow-up session for participants to share their observations of children's play in the house corner.

Handout # 1: Observing Dramatic Play

Observe children in the house corner over a one week period. Note examples of how their play contributes to the following developmental areas.

Social Development:

Emotional Development:

Physical Development:

Cognitive Development:

The Role of Props in Dramatic Play

Participants in this workshop will:

* explore a variety of props and materials that can be added to the house corner;

* act out a series of role plays to illustrate the value of props in stimulating dramatic play; and

* learn about prop boxes.

Materials needed:

* Chart pad, markers, and tape

* An assortment of interesting props to explore, such as an alarm clock, a radio (without wires), a cordless shaver, a cordless hair dryer, an old toaster, gauze-like fabric in bright colors, white sheets, a briefcase or suitcase, a sleeping bag, a stamp pad and paper, a hole punch, shopping bags, and so forth

Handouts:

* "Role Play Cards" (Handout #2)

* "Using Prop Boxes in the House Corner" (Handout #3)

Activity: Exploring Props for the House Corner

Explain that a variety of items can be used for props in the house corner. Divide participants into four groups and ask each to explore the props you have laid out on four separate tables. Have them discuss how they think children would use these props and what types of dramatic play themes the props might stimulate. Allow about 10 minutes for the exercise. Have each group share the highlights of their discussion. In summarizing the experience, be sure to make the following points:

* Children's dramatic play is greatly stimulated by the props and materials available.

* All props should be in good repair, attractive, and in sufficient quantities (e.g., two or three baby dolls, two suitcases, etc.).

* Many props for the house corner can be donated by parents or purchased in a second-hand store.

Role Play: How Props Support Dramatic Play

Explain that this exercise will give participants a chance to experience the importance of props in dramatic play. Divide participants into groups of four or five. Ask for two volunteers in each group to role play a brief scene. Give each set of volunteers the role play cards. The directions are to read the card and act out the role without talking. The remaining group members will have to guess what is happening.

Allow about two minutes for the role play. Then, without commenting, place the props in front of the "players." Allow the role play to continue until the other participants can guess the scene.

Conclude the exercise by asking the following questions:

- "Was it hard to play the role without any props? Why?"

- "How did the props help?"

- "When props were added, did the role play last longer?"

- "What other props might have been fun to use?"

Summarize the discussion by emphasizing that children respond in similar ways to props:

- When interesting and varied props are available, dramatic play scenes usually last longer.

- Realistic props help children act out familiar roles and experiences.

- The more varied and creative the props, the more creative and involved dramatic play can become.

Activity: Creating Prop Boxes to Stimulate Dramatic Play

Explain that an important part of the teacher's role is to extend play in the house corner by introducing new dramatic play themes. Ask participants when it might be appropriate to introduce new themes, and list their responses on the chart. You might hear the following:

- Introduce new themes when children seem bored with the house corner or avoid the area.

- A new theme can build on children's current experiences (e.g., the birth of a new baby; a child moving; a visit to the fire station).

Introduce the idea of prop boxes and explain that they contain materials that will stimulate children's dramatic play with regard to a particular place or adult role. For example, a collection of materials that stimulate children to play hospital or doctor/nurse.

Lead a discussion of what could be included in a prop box for an office. Write the suggestions on a chart. (See the House Corner module for suggestions.)

Be sure to make the following points:

- A prop box should include something that triggers the children's memory about a particular place or adult role (e.g., a stethoscope means the doctor's office, a hat or part of a uniform relates to a community helper, a sign such as golden arches means McDonald's, etc.).

- A prop box should be placed in the house corner where the children can see what is inside and should be there before they arrive. The materials themselves will stimulate the children's play; the teacher will not have to prompt them to use the materials.

- Sometimes it is helpful to use a prop box in conjunction with reading a particular story or returning from a field trip; children especially enjoy acting out roles they have just seen.

- A variety of prop boxes can be assembled and "rotated" in the house corner; several can be available for children to use and new ones can be introduced every few months.

Assignment

End the discussion by distributing Handout #3, "Using Prop Boxes in the House Corner." Ask participants to create a prop box for their own classroom, place it in the house corner, and observe the children using the prop box. (If participants need help choosing a prop box theme, refer them to the appropriate section of the House Corner module in the *Creative Curriculum* for suggestions.)

Handout #2: Role Play Cards

Photocopy and cut out each role play and paste it onto a 3 x 5 index card.

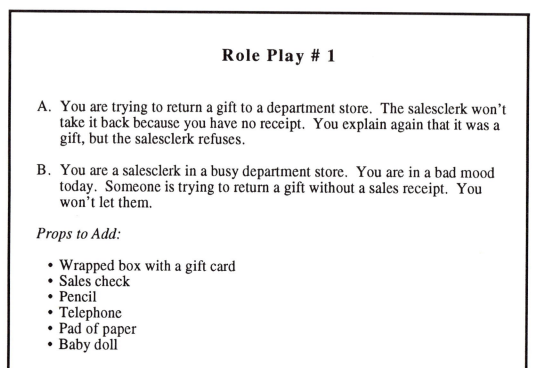

Role Play # 1

A. You are trying to return a gift to a department store. The salesclerk won't take it back because you have no receipt. You explain again that it was a gift, but the salesclerk refuses.

B. You are a salesclerk in a busy department store. You are in a bad mood today. Someone is trying to return a gift without a sales receipt. You won't let them.

Props to Add:

- Wrapped box with a gift card
- Sales check
- Pencil
- Telephone
- Pad of paper
- Baby doll

Role Play # 2

A. You are riding the bus to your new job for the first time. You don't know where to get off. You try to ask the bus driver for help.

B. You are a bus driver. A passenger who is lost is trying to find out which stop is nearest to her new job. You try to help her.

Props to Add:

- Maps
- Driver's hat
- Watch
- Shopping bag

Handout #3: Using Prop Boxes in the House Corner

Name of Your Prop Box: _____

Items Included:_____

    _____

    _____

    _____

    _____

    _____

    _____

    _____

    _____

    _____

Place the prop box you created in the house corner. Observe the children and record what they do with the materials. Pay close attention to what they say. Give specific examples.

Follow-Up on Using Prop Boxes

> **Participants in this workshop will:**
>
> - share the prop boxes they made for their classroom; and
>
> - review their observations of how children used the prop boxes.

Materials needed:

- Chart pad, markers, and tape

- Prop boxes created by participants

- Completed Handout #3, "Using Prop Boxes in the House Corner"

Handout:

- "Levels of Ability in Dramatic Play" (Handout #4)

Discussion: Sharing of Experiences Using Prop Boxes

Allow time for participants to share the contents of their prop boxes and to discuss what they collected, how they prepared the prop boxes, and how children used them in dramatic play. You might ask questions such as the following:

- "How did you introduce the prop box?"

- "What did the children do with the props?" "Did they ask for additional props?"

- "What other types of prop boxes would be appropriate for the children in your group?"

- "How could you use prop boxes to introduce curriculum themes?"

End by suggesting that participants use prop boxes and other materials to convert the house corner into another "stage" for play (e.g., a hospital, a hotel, airport, grocery store, etc.) and leave it up for one week. Also suggest that they observe the house corner in another program to gain additional ideas.

Assignment:

Distribute Handout #4, "Levels of Ability in Dramatic Play." Review the form and answer any questions participants have about how and when to complete the observation. Ask them to bring the completed form to the next session.

Handout #4: Levels of Ability in Dramatic Play

Select one child to observe in the house corner for several days. Use the following questions to guide your observation/completion of the form on the following pages.

Role Playing

- What role(s) does the child play?

- What type of role is this (family member, animal, monster, self, etc.)?

- Does the child select the same role day after day or experiment with different roles?

- How many different aspects of the role does the child play?

Use of Props

- Does the child use props?

- Which props does the child use? Clothes? Hats? Tools? Dolls? Furniture?

- How does the child use the props? Is the child interested in the prop and what it can do, or does the prop merely serve as set decoration?

- How many different props does the child use?

- Does the child think of creative ideas for props, such as using a string of beads to represent spaghetti and meatballs?

Use of Make-Believe

- Does the child's play include fantasy?

- Are the elements of fantasy used by the child simple or complex in structure?

- Do you think the child's ideas for make-believe come from stories, from TV, or from the child's own imagination?

Use of Time

- How much time does the child spend involved in a dramatic play episode?

- How much of the child's time is spent in group play?

- Which play themes hold the child's attention longest?

- How persistent is the child in carrying out the role selected?

Interaction

- Does the child play alone? With one other child? As part of a group?

- Who initiates group play? Is it always the same child who assigns roles and gets things started?

- How does the child let other children know of interest in group play?

- How does the child resolve problems in sharing props, selecting roles, and giving directions?

Verbal Communication

- What does the child say during play?

- Does the child use language to communicate ideas? Give directions? Explain things? Ask for information? Request props?

- Does the child's voice sound different when taking on a role than when speaking normally?

OBSERVATION FORM

Criteria	Beginning Level	Advanced Level
(1) Role Play (a) Role chosen		
(b) How child plays role		
(2) Using Props (a) Type of prop needed		
(b) How child uses props		

OBSERVATION FORM (Continued)

Criteria	Beginning Level	Advanced Level
(3) Make-Believe		
(4) Time		
(5) Interaction		
(6) Verbal Communication		

The Teacher's Role

Participants in this workshop will:

- use their observations of children in the house corner to identify levels of dramatic play; and

- identify ways to support and extend dramatic play in the house corner.

Materials needed:

- Chart pad, markers, and tape

- Completed observation on Handout #4

- *The Creative Curriculum* videotape and VCR

Discussion: Identifying Levels of Dramatic Play

Begin by reiterating why observations are so valuable. Ask participants for reasons and record them on the chart pad. Be sure to include the following:

- Observing children in the house corner helps adults better understand how children interpret relationships among the people in the world around them.

- Because children typically play together in the house corner, teachers have a unique opportunity to observe emerging socialization skills.

- Observing children at play allows teachers to assess children's use of language.

- Children are helped to deal with their fears and other powerful emotions through dramatic play; teachers can observe ways in which individual children cope with their feelings.

- Observations enable teachers to identify where children are, developmentally.

Next, review the observation form that participants have completed on levels of ability in dramatic play. Go through each category and have participants cite examples of what they observed. You might ask questions such as the following:

- "What dramatic play themes did children develop?"

- "What roles have you seen children play?"

- "What examples can you give of children at the beginning level? Advanced level?"

- "What props are typically used by children at the beginning level? Advanced level?"

- "How long do children at each level remain engaged in a play theme? Do props extend the amount of time that children continue a theme?"

Summarize the discussion by pointing out that knowing individual children's developmental level enables teachers to respond appropriately to each child's needs. Do children need more props? Should they be encouraged to move to the next developmental stage? Are they "stuck" in their choice of dramatic play roles?

Videotape: *The Creative Curriculum*

Show the house corner portion of *The Creative Curriculum* videotape. Ask participants to focus on when teachers intervene and what kind of questions they ask. Note that the videotape shows teachers interacting with children in the following scenes:

- a restaurant;
- a space capsule;
- caring for a baby;
- a shoe store; and
- a teacher-made car.

Activity: Interacting with Children in the House Corner

Divide participants into groups of four or five. Ask them to use their own observations as a basis for developing strategies for teacher intervention to extend and enrich dramatic play. For example:

A three-year-old brings the teacher a cup and says, "here." To extend the play and stimulate conversation and language development, the teacher might say, "What's in the cup?" or "Thank you! Do you have some milk in the refrigerator for me?"

Refer participants to the House Corner module for suggestions on the teacher's role.

Allow as much time as needed; then have each group share their suggestions and list them on the flip chart. Summarize the discussion by including the following points:

- Asking open-ended questions is a good way to extend dramatic play.

- Adding new props will extend dramatic play themes.

- The teacher's role is to intervene without interfering with children's dramatic play.

V. Table Toy Workshops

A well-organized, protected, and richly stocked table toy area offers many opportunities for children to work alone or with a friend on a discrete task. Too often, however, the table toy area is ignored by both children and staff. Teachers involve themselves in more active areas—blocks or art—and leave children on their own with table toys. Children become bored when they see the same toys on the shelves week after week, and so they select other more interesting and challenging activities.

Workshops on table toys can inspire teachers and parents to look at these manipulative materials in a new way. The workshops outlined in this section are designed to give participants an opportunity to stretch their thinking, solve problems, explore, and devise new and creative ways to use common materials and toys.

Workshops: **Page**

The Importance of Table Toys 114

Evaluating Table Toys 117

The Teacher's Role 123

Handouts:

"Sandola Plants" (Handout #1) 116

"Form for Evaluating Table Toys" (Handout #2) 119

"Table Toy Observation Form" (Handout #3) 121

The Importance of Table Toys

Participants in this workshop will:

• learn how table toys stimulate children's thinking and problem-solving skills;

• identify the three major types of table toys; and

• discuss ways to display table toys in the classroom.

Materials needed:

• Chart pad and markers

• Slide/Videotape: *The New Room Arrangement as a Teaching Strategy*

• Colored plastic bottle caps of varying shapes, sizes, and types; a variety of buttons in several sizes, colors, and shapes; plastic bread bag fasteners in different sizes and colors; seashells, keys

Handout:

• "Sandola Plants" (Handout #1)

Activity: Promoting Thinking Skills

Distribute the handout "Sandola Plants" and review the directions, asking participants to try to figure out which of the 'plants' on the bottom of the page will grow on the planet Sandola.

Allow participants time to solve the problem and then ask:

• "Who has the answer?"

• "What did you have to do to solve the problem?"

(The answer is numbers 2 and 4 because they have the same three characteristics as all of the "plants" on the first line: there is something inside the head of each plant, there is something on top of their heads, and the body of each plant is facing left.)

If participants seem to be having trouble with the task, you might ask:

• "What characteristics do the 'plants' in row one have in common?"

• "Which of the 'plants' in row three have all of the same characteristics as the 'plants' in row one?"

Point out that the purpose of the exercise is to focus on problem solving and thinking skills. When children play with table toys, there are many opportunities to develop these skills.

Next, pass around your collection of bottle caps and ask each participant to select a cap to examine. Then say:

- "Look at the bottle cap carefully and identify all of its characteristics."

- "Now find someone who has a cap that's like yours in one way."

- "Can you form a group of three caps?"

- "Now see how many ways you can develop new groups of caps."

Summarize the exercise by reviewing what participants need to do and know to complete the task (i.e., identify similarities and differences and classify or group objects accordingly). Learning to classify like objects is an important thinking skill that children develop and refine when they play with table toys.

Have participants form groups of four each. Give each group a set of "collectibles" (e.g., keys, buttons, plastic bread bag fasteners, seashells). Their task is to figure out as many ways as possible to group the objects.

Allow approximately 10 minutes for the activity and then ask each group to share their categories. Summarize the foregoing activities by suggesting that participants make these or other "collectibles" available in the classroom and see what children do with them.

Slide/Videotape: *The New Room Arrangement as a Teaching Strategy*

Introduce the presentation by noting that the way in which materials are organized and displayed will influence what children select and how they use table toys.

Show the slide/videotape and ask participants to particularly note appropriate and inappropriate examples of how to organize and display table toys.

After viewing the slide/videotape presentation, ask if anyone has used the ideas presented in organizing their table toy area. Encourage participants to share their experiences. If appropriate for your group, allow time for participants to make labels for their table toy areas. Be sure to have sufficient quantities of cardboard, magic markers, construction paper, scissors, toy catalogues, and clear contact paper. Or you can ask participants to make labels as an assignment and bring them to the next session to share.

Assignment:

Refer participants to the module on Table Toys in the *Creative Curriculum* that defines three types of table toys: self-correcting toys, open-ended toys, and collectibles. Ask participants to give examples of toys from their classroom that fit into each category. For the next session, ask each participant to bring in an example from each category to share with the group.

Handout #1: Sandola Plants

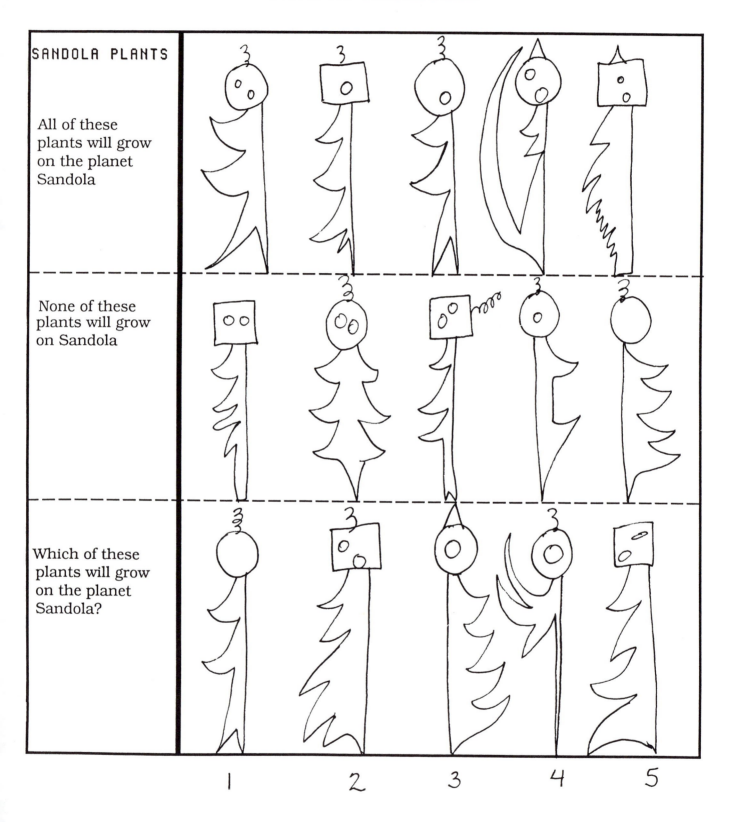

Evaluating Table Toys

Participants in this workshop will:

- explore a variety of table toys;

- use a set of criteria to evaluate table toys; and

- identify the skills and concepts that children learn playing with various table toys and how to extend their use.

Materials needed:

- Chart pad and markers

- Tables for displaying table toys

- Table toys including: peg board and pegs, stringing beads, colored cubes, lotto game, puzzles, nesting toy, parquetry blocks, sewing cards, Legos

Handouts:

- "Evaluating Table Toys" (Handout #2)

- "Table Toy Observation" (Handout #3)

Activity: Evaluating Table Toys

Introduce the workshop by explaining that participants will have an opportunity to explore and critique a wide variety of table toys. Invite participants to share the table toys and collectibles they have brought to the workshop. Distribute the form for "Evaluating Table Toys" (Handout #2) and review each question briefly. (Refer participants to the module on Table Toys for definitions of the criteria listed in question 3.)

Ask participants to evaluate the toys at their table answering questions 1-5 on the form.   Allow approximately 10 minutes for the task.

Give each group a chance to explain how it categorized and evaluated its table toys.   In summarizing the participants' comments, include the following points:

- Table toys are often structured to be used in certain ways.

- Table toys should always be age appropriate, that is, challenging without being too simple or too complex.

- Children at different stages will use the same toys in different ways. For instance, a two-year-old will most likely stack nesting blocks and a four-year-old may use them to create a design or a setting for dramatic play.

- Toys should meet the criteria for safety and durability.

- All toys should be nonracist and nonsexist. When evaluating table toys with pictures (e.g., lotto games, family doll sets), it is important to be sure that people are not portrayed in stereotypical ways.

Activity: What Children Learn from Table Toys

Using the same toys, have participants answer questions 6 to 8 on the form for "Evaluating Table Toys." For question 6, ask for specific examples of how the toy helps to promote physical, cognitive, and social/emotional development. Allow approximately 15 minutes for this task.

In reviewing the list of examples, refer to the goals and objectives for table toys in the *Creative Curriculum*.

Assignment:

Distribute the form for "Table Toy Observation" (Handout #3) and review it briefly. Ask participants to complete the form and bring it to the next session.

Handout #2: Form for Evaluating Table Toys

1. Type of toy:

   (a) Is it a "self-correcting, structured" toy? (That is, is it a toy that fits together in a certain way so the children know when they have finished and when they have done it correctly?)

   (b) Is it "open-ended?" (That is, is it a toy that can be put together in many different ways so that each time a child plays with it, something new can be made?)

   (c) Collectibles:

   What are some open-ended ways in which these can be used?

2. Does the toy meet the following criteria?

	Yes	No	Why Not
Safety			
Durability			
Construction			
Flexibility			

3.   Is the toy nonsexist? What messages are conveyed about what men and women can do?

4.   Is the toy nonracist?   Does it convey positive images of ethnic groups and portray people in nonstereotypical roles?

5.   What age group(s) do you think this toy is appropriate for?

6.   Which concepts or skills could children learn when using this toy?

7.   What would you expect children to do with this toy? List all of the possible ideas children might invent for using the toy. How would you structure and guide children's use of the table toy?

8.   What new ideas can you think of for using this toy? How can you extend its use?

Handout # 3: Table Toy Observation

Introduction

Before determining an appropriate strategy for interacting with children in the table toy area, it's important to know which toys and materials the children are selecting and what they do with the materials they choose. You also need to know how often individual children use the table toy area and whether they play alone or with other children. This information provides you with a basis on which to make decisions so that you can respond appropriately to children's interests and needs.

Part I

Select a time during free play to observe the table toy area for 10 to 15 minutes, over the course of one week.

1.   How many children use the table toy area each day?

2.   Which toys do the children select most often?

3.   Are there any table toys that the children tend to ignore? What are they, and why do you think this is the case?

4.   Do children tend to play alone or in groups? Give some examples.

5.   Do some toys lend themselves more to solitary play? Group play?

6.   Are there any toys that you need more of? Less of? Why?

Part II

Select one child to observe in the table toy area and record the following:

1.   What toys does the child select?

2.   What does the child do with the table toy(s)?

3.   Is the child playing alone or with a friend?

4.   What examples do you see of ways that the child's play contributes to:

     Social/emotional development?

     Physical development?

     Cognitive development?

The Teacher's Role

Participants in this workshop will:

- develop techniques to expand and extend what children do with table toys;

- explore the value of supplementing the table toy area with homemade materials; and/or

- make table toys for their classroom.

Materials needed:

- Chart pad and markers

- Participants' completed "Table Toy Observation" form

- Table toys: those used for earlier sessions plus examples of the homemade table toys that participants create

- *The Creative Curriculum* videotape and VCR

Discussion: Observing Children in the Table Toy Area

Lead the participants in a review of their classroom observations by asking the following questions:

- "What did you see children doing with table toys?"

- "Which toys are most popular? Why do you think this is so?"

- "Were the toys age appropriate? Did they hold the children's interest?"

- "In what ways were children challenged by the toys?"

- "Did you observe children using table toys in creative or unexpected ways?"

Summarize the observation exercise by asking participants to identify one change they would like to make in their table toy area, based on what they observed.

Activity: Teaching Strategies for the Table Toy Area

Form groups of three or four and have each group select two toys to explore. Ask each group to complete the following tasks:

- Identify how you would interest a child in each toy.

- Prepare a list of closed questions and another list of open-ended questions you could ask about the toys.

- Identify new ways and/or games you could make up using each toy.

Allow approximately 30 minutes for the exercise. In reviewing the group's strategies, refer to the module on Table Toys and include some of the examples provided.

Videotape: *The Creative Curriculum*

Show the portion of the videotape on table toys and have participants note how the area is set up, what children are learning in the table toy area, and how teachers intervene.

Discussion: The Value of Homemade Table Toys

On the chart pad, list some of the advantages of supplementing the table toy area with homemade materials:

- They can be tailored to meet the needs of children in your group.

- They can be designed to teach and reinforce a specific skill or concept.

- They are an inexpensive way to supplement the table toy area.

- A variety of "collectibles" greatly enriches the table toy area.

At this point in the workshop, you can either:

- provide materials and have participants make their own table toys; or

- assign the task of making a table toy and schedule a follow-up session so participants can share the toys they have made.

VI. Art Workshops

The primary purpose of conducting workshops on art is to give participants an opportunity to explore art materials and learn firsthand why the *Creative Curriculum* emphasizes the process rather than the product that results from children's play in the art area.

A workshop approach is particularly effective for conveying the underlying values of art for young children. Giving teachers and parents an opportunity to explore different art media allows them to get in touch with their own creativity. As a result, they are better able to support children's explorations and to encourage their creative ideas.

Workshops: **Page**

The Importance of Art 126

Setting Up the Art Area: The Physical Environment 130

The Teacher's Role 133

Handout:

"Sergeant Pepper Coloring Design" 129

The Importance of Art

Participants in this workshop will:

- define creativity and why it is important;

- identify the value of art experiences;

- experience an inappropriate art activity; and

- identify barriers to successful art experiences.

Materials needed:

- Chart pad, markers, and tape

- Crayons—a sufficient quantity for the group

Handout:

- "Sergeant Pepper Coloring Design"

Discussion: The Importance of Creativity

Note that in the *Creative Curriculum*, the focus is on process: what children do in the art area rather than the final product. Ask participants how they would describe a creative person.

Brainstorm with participants to generate a list of ideas; record all responses. In summarizing the discussion, you may want to highlight the following points:

- Creativity means looking at things in a unique and original way.

- People who are creative look for more than one way to do something or solve a problem; they can think of many options.

- Creative people exhibit qualities such as spontaneity, originality, a willingness to take risks, flexibility, and a sense of adventure.

- Creative people feel secure in their opinions and ideas.

Point out that these are all qualities that we want to encourage in young children. Although creativity is encouraged in all areas of the *Creative Curriculum*, it receives particular emphasis in the art experiences we plan. By their very nature, art materials provide excellent opportunities for children to explore, experiment, and use their imaginations.

Discussion: The Value of Art Experiences for Young Children

Divide the participants into groups of four or five. Ask participants to discuss the following, on the basis of their experiences in the classroom:

- "Why do children enjoy using art materials?"

- "What do children gain from exploring and experimenting with art materials?"

Allow 10 to 15 minutes and record the groups' responses on the chart pad. You might hear that in using art materials, children:

- experience a sense of accomplishment;

- put their ideas into concrete form;

- express their feelings and views of the world;

- refine physical skills—small muscle development and eye/hand coordination;

- learn concepts such as size, shape, and color;

- have opportunities to develop social skills; and

- make choices, work independently, try out new ideas, and experiment.

Explain that there are many ways that teachers can encourage creativity in children's art. These will be discussed later in the workshop and will include:

- setting up the classroom in ways that support successful experiences in art;

- selecting and displaying age-appropriate art materials;

- talking to children using art materials; and

- encouraging children's art and enriching their experiences.

Activity: A Developmentally Inappropriate Exercise

To demonstrate how young children feel when art activities are inappropriate, distribute the "Sergeant Pepper" handout and provide crayons for participants. Give the following directions:

- Select a color you like.

- If you are right handed, put the crayon in your left hand; if you are left handed, put the crayon in your right hand.

- Now color in the design as quickly as you can and stay in the lines.

As participants are working on the coloring assignment, walk around the room and make comments such as the following:

- "Try a little harder to stay in the lines."

- "Look how nicely Trudy is coloring her design."

- "Hurry up and complete the task."

- "Have you ever seen anyone with green hair?"

After several minutes of this activity, participants will probably express their frustrations freely. Now distribute a blank sheet of paper and tell participants that they can color whatever they would like, with as many different crayons/colors as they wish.

After they are finished, lead a discussion by asking:

- "What did you experience in the second activity?" (i.e., freedom, large movement, fun).

- "What did you experience in the first activity?" (i.e., pressure, boredom, having to work hard to please the teacher).

Ask participants to identify the advantages of child-initiated art and the advantages of coloring books. Record the ideas on a chart. It may look something like the one below.

Child-initiated art	Coloring books (Sgt. Pepper handout)
Express their own ideas Organize space Experience a sense of pride (I can do it myself) Use color freely Represent their ideas on paper (reading and math readiness)	Learn to stay in the lines Develop small muscle control Follow directions

Conclude the discussion by stating that coloring books are not considered a creative art activity. Although children may use them at times, they should not be part of the art area.

Discussion: Barriers to Successful Art Experiences

Teachers often experience some problems in making the art area a successful place for learning. Lead participants in a discussion to identify what they feel are the barriers to a good art program. Begin by asking:

"What are some typical problems you experience in making the art area work well for you and for the children?"

Record participants' ideas on chart paper. Teachers often describe problems such as the following:

- There isn't enough room to store art supplies.
- There aren't enough materials.
- Art activities can be very messy.
- There isn't enough space for art in the classroom.
- When we paint, the children all want to use the easel at the same time.
- During art the children get their clothes stained and the parents complain.
- When we're doing art, I end up doing all the work.
- The children don't help with clean-up and it takes forever to clean the paint brushes.

Explain that the following workshops will address these issues. Ask participants to bring to the next workshop a floor plan of their classroom and a list of art supplies.

Sergeant Pepper Coloring Design

Setting Up the Art Area: The Physical Environment

Participants in this workshop will:

•   review floor plans of their own classrooms and identify changes they want to make in the location and arrangement of their art area;

•   learn new ways to display and organize art materials; and

•   identify basic art supplies and materials for a preschool program.

Materials needed:

•   Floor plans of participants' classrooms

•   Cardboard, markers, and clear contact paper to make labels (optional)

•   Sample display containers and labels for art materials

Small Group Activity: Review of Floor Plans

Explain that many of the problems identified at the last workshop can be eliminated by proper location of the art area and by an appealing and orderly arrangement and display of art materials. Invite participants to work in pairs to share their floor plans. List the following questions on chart paper for them to consider:

•   Would a new child coming into your classroom know where art activities take place?

•   What other activities take place near the art area?

•   Where do you keep the art materials that children can select and use?

•   Where do you store extra supplies and teachers' materials?

•   Do children know where to find art materials and how to return them to the proper place?

Bring the group together and lead a discussion on guidelines for setting up the art area. Emphasize the following points:

•   There should be a designated area for art in the classroom that children can easily identify.

•   The art area should be closed in on three sides; use shelves and walls to create space.

- The art area should be located out of the line of traffic so that children will be able to work without bumping into each other.

- Whenever possible, the art area should be near the source of water in the classroom; if this is not possible, buckets of water can be set up along with paper towels for washing hands and paint brushes.

- The art area should have enough space for children to work comfortably and should include a table, floor space, and easels. The table should be large enough to accommodate four children who can work without crowding each other.

Have participants review their floor plans and identify what changes, if any, they wish to make in the location and arrangement of their art areas.

Discussion and Activity: Selecting, Displaying, and Labeling Materials in the Art Area

Lead a discussion on the basic materials needed for an art program. Using the categories suggested in the *Creative Curriculum*, have participants identify what materials they have in each category.

- Something to paint on (an easel with paper)

- Something to paint with (brushes and paints)

- Something to draw with (crayons and markers)

- Something to draw on (a variety of paper)

- Something that puts things together (paste and glue)

- Something for cutting (scissors)

- Something to mold (clay or play dough)

- Something to clean up with (sponge, broom, mop, paper towels, and water)

Refer participants to the list of basic art supplies in the *Creative Curriculum* and the list of suggested supplemental art supplies. Again, you can have participants identify materials they have collected and used for art. They can prepare a list of materials they intend to add to their art areas.

Show participants the sample containers you have brought for displaying art materials. The module on Art in the *Creative Curriculum* contains illustrated descriptions of how to display and store art materials. Highlight some of the following guidelines:

- Basic art materials should be grouped together by their function, (e.g., collage materials, glue and scissors, crayons and paper).

- Supplemental art materials can be stored in a closet or on a high bookshelf until needed. A curtain in front of an open cupboard will keep supplies and teacher's materials out of view of the children.

- Storage containers such as sturdy shoe boxes, fruit baskets, or plastic tubs are useful for storing extra art materials. It's helpful to label each container so you can find what you need.

- Pockets can be useful, too. You can use an old hanging shoe bag or make your own: cover a sheet of plywood or tri-wall with colorful material such as burlap or heavy felt. Staple pieces of plastic, acetate, or heavy felt to it to make pockets, and hang it on the inside door of the teachers' storage area.

Share sample labels for art materials and discuss the value of labeling. Stress the following points:

- Labeled shelves help children learn where to find materials and where to put them back.

- You can make labels for the art area in several ways—by drawing a picture of the material, taking a photograph, or including a sample of the real object.

- Labels covered with clean contact paper last longer.

- Picture labels should be displayed directly on the shelf where materials will be stored. Containers used for storage can have the label attached to the outside of the container.

- In addition to the picture label, four- and five-year-olds like to identify the written word next to the picture label.

Set out materials needed for making labels so that participants who have not labeled their art area can do so at the workshop.

The Teacher's Role

Participants in this workshop will:

- collect and share drawings and paintings made by young children and identify developmental stages;

- participate in a variety of art activities appropriate for young children; and

- learn what to say to children involved in art experiences.

Materials needed:

- A room large enough to accommodate four tables, each with a different art activity

- Collections of children's drawings and paintings (ask participants to bring these to the workshop)

- Painting materials:

  something to paint on (e.g., free-standing easel or wall easel with paper or a table with paper)

  tools to paint with (e.g., brushes)

  paint in primary colors

  paint holders (see the *Creative Curriculum*)

- Collage and assemblage materials:

  a variety of scrap materials

  small blocks of wood, small cardboard boxes, or styrofoam or meat trays to serve as an assemblage base

  paste and glue

  heavy paper such as cardboard or construction paper

  scissors

- Drawing materials:

  various types of paper
  crayons, felt, and markers
  white and colored chalk

- Clay and playdough:

    ingredients for homemade playdough (see recipes in the *Creative Curriculum*)

    prepared playdough

    modeling clay

    props such as small rolling pins, cookie cutters, and tongue depressors

    coffee cans to store the playdough

- Clean up materials:

    broom, sponges, water, and paper towels

- *The Creative Curriculum* videotape and VCR

Introduction: Developmental Stages in Children's Art

Have participants share the drawings and paintings they have collected from their children. You can do this by age group—threes, fours, and fives—or place all the pictures on a table and ask participants to try to guess the age of the child who made each one. Refer participants to the developmental stages illustrated in the module on Art.

Activity: Exploring Art Materials

Explain that during this part of the workshop, participants will have a chance to experiment with some of the art materials children particularly enjoy. While they are working, you will be assuming the role of the "teacher" to demonstrate how to extend learning. Encourage participants to talk about what they are doing as they work with the materials.

Invite participants to select whatever activity they want to try. They can spend the full time on one activity or try them all.

While participants are working, rotate from one area to another and take notes on what you hear people saying as they work with materials. For example, you might hear comments such as the following:

- "This playdough is mushy."
- "This is fun."
- "My paint is globbing."
- "I need more..."
- "What happens if I..."
- "Look what I did!"

Comment on the participants' efforts by using words and phrases that you want them to use with the children.

- "Would you like to tell me about your picture?"
- "How did you make purple? I didn't give you that color."
- "How could you make the playdough less sticky?"
- "Can you tell me how you did this?"

Give the group a five-minute warning before you plan to conclude the activity. Model how you would do this in the classroom.

- "You have just enough time to finish that painting before it's time to move to clean up."

- "Think about what else you want to add to your collage, because in a few minutes we'll have to move on to something else."

Discussion: Review of the Activity

Ask participants to describe their experiences using the various art materials. You can record their answers on chart paper as they respond to questions such as the following:

- "What did you like about each of the activities you tried?"
- "What discoveries did you make?"
- "What could children learn?"

Develop a list of responses for each of the art experiences you provided.

Share with participants the comments they made and what you noticed as they explored the art materials. Relate your observations to what teachers should be looking for when they observe children in the art area. For example, teachers should note:

- what materials children select;
- how children use the materials;
- whether children work alone or with others;
- how long children remain at a task;
- what fine motor skills they have developed; and
- whether they are ready for more challenging art experiences.

Small Group Activity: Talking with Children about Their Artwork

Begin the discussion by asking participants what they noticed about the comments you made to them as they explored the art materials. Point out that your comments focused on the process and that you avoided making judgments. You described what you observed, for example:

- what colors they used;
- their actions in exploring the materials;
- the problems they encountered and solved; and
- their discoveries.

You avoided saying:

- "What color is this?"
- "That's pretty."
- "What did you make?"
- "Try not to use so much glue."

In addition to describing what children are doing, teachers should ask open-ended questions to encourage children to think and express their ideas. Explain that the next activity is designed to give participants practice in asking open-ended questions.

Organize four groups, one for each of the art activity areas. Ask each group to come up with a list of open-ended questions that teachers could ask to extend children's thinking. For example:

- Painting

    "What would happen if you didn't wipe your paint brush?"

    "Would you like to tell me about your painting?"

    "You made a new color at the easel! How did you do it?"

- Collage

    "How did you get that straw to stay up?"

    "Which glue works best?"

- Drawing

    "What happened when you dipped the chalk in the starch?"

    "Tell me something about your picture."

    "You have been working hard; tell me about what you have been doing."

- Clay and playdough

    "How can we make the dough less sticky?"

    "What would happen if we added more water to the clay?"

Give each group a chance to share their list of open-ended questions. You may want to duplicate the lists and provide each participant with a copy following the workshop.

Videotape: *The Creative Curriculum*

To conclude the workshop, show the portion of the videotape on art. There are several good examples of how teachers facilitate problem solving in the art area. You may want to call participants' attention to the following scenes they will see on the videotape:

- A child using tape to hold an assemblage together
- The finger painting scene where the paint is too thin to hold a handprint
- The clay scene
- The child building a tower that won't stand up
- An outdoor painting scene

Allow time after showing the videotape for participants to discuss their impressions.

VII. Sand and Water Workshops

It's not uncommon for teachers to avoid offering sand and water play activities in the classroom. Focusing on the added clean-up involved, they fail to consider the wide range of learning opportunities and the developmental advantages of these natural materials.

Sand and water are soothing materials that appeal to children's need for sensory stimulation. Children become scientists and mathematicians playing with sand and water—learning the properties of each, measuring, comparing, trying out experiments, and using their imaginations. The sand and water area can become a rich setting for learning, even on the most limited budget.

The purpose of providing workshops on sand and water is to help teachers and parents appreciate the value of these materials in children's learning and development.

Workshops: **Page**

Creating Learning Opportunities with Sand and Water 138

Exploring Math and Science Concepts with Sand and Water 141

Creating Learning Opportunities with Sand and Water

> **Participants in this workshop will:**
>
> • explore the properties of sand and water; and
>
> • explore a variety of props for sand and water play.

Materials needed:

- Chart pad and markers

- Water table and/or individual plastic tubs

- Sand table and/or individual plastic tubs

- Warm and cold water in plastic containers

- Fine and course sand

- Food coloring

- Dishwashing liquid detergent

- Sawdust

- Rice, beans, or oatmeal (see caution on using food in the *Creative Curriculum*)

- Props for sand and water play (e.g., plastic tubing, egg beaters, bulb syringes, small paint brushes, medicine droppers, corks, ping-pong balls, troughs, ropes, rolling pins, seashells and cookie cutters, magnifying glasses, sieves, colanders, funnels, weighing scales)

- Clean-up supplies (e.g., brooms, mops, sponges, paper towels, dust pan)

Setting up:

Whenever possible, try to conduct the workshops in a classroom so you can demonstrate where to locate sand and water play, how to set up activities, and how to facilitate clean-up.

If sand and water tables are available, they can accommodate three to four adults for the workshop. In addition, you can provide plastic tubs or basins. This will demonstrate alternatives to the larger sand and water tables. If you don't have sand and water tables, be sure to provide enough basins or tubs so that participants have room to explore the materials.

Before the session begins, set up the sand and water tables and individual basins. Place warm and cold water in plastic containers. Next to each water basin, place food coloring and liquid soap. Fill the sand table and bins with both fine and coarse sand, if possible. Provide additional bins with rice, beans, uncooked oatmeal, and sawdust for comparison. Have clean-up supplies on hand to demonstrate ways to include children in clean-up activities.

Activity: Exploring Sand and Water

Ask participants to think for a minute about their own experiences with sand and water.

- "Close your eyes and imagine you are at the beach."

- "How does the beach feel? Look? Smell? Sound? Taste?"

- "What do you like to do at the beach?"

In discussing participants' responses, point out that sand and water are natural materials that appeal to our senses: touch, smell, sound, and sight. Children and adults alike are drawn to sand and water. Using them is relaxing, pleasurable, and soothing. In addition, sand and water play offer many opportunities for children to learn new concepts and enhance their social and physical skills.

Form groups of three or four participants and provide a water and sand table or basin for each group. Begin with the water and the following directions:

- "Start with just plain water and see how far you can go exploring its properties."

- "Now, add the liquid soap and/or food coloring and see what happens."

Allow 5 to 10 minutes for the activity. Explain that you want everyone to explore water without props first to see all the possibilities of the material by itself. Ask questions that encourage participants to share their experience and discoveries.

- "How does water sound? Feel? Look?"

- "Does water have a temperature?"

- "What happened when you added soap? Food coloring? How did the water change?"

You may hear comments such as the following:

- The temperature of water affects the experience.
- Water sounds hard when you slap it.
- Water whooshes.
- Water feels soft.
- Water seems quiet/fast/slow.
- Water is clear/cloudy/plain/soapy.
- Bubbles fly/burst/explode.
- Water makes waves.

To summarize the experience, note that exploration with water by itself enables children to discover its many properties. When props are added, children can experiment even more.

Next, repeat the exploration exercise for sand. Ask the groups to explore the different types of sand provided and to compare them with the other substances (e.g., beans, sawdust, uncooked oatmeal).

Lead the participants in a discussion of what they discovered about sand. You might ask:

- "How does sand feel? Look?"

- "How does your experience change when using coarse sand? How are the two kinds the same? How are they different?"

- "What can you do to sand?"

- "How does sand differ from the other substances? Are they alike in any ways?"

You might hear:

- Sand is cool/warm.
- Sand is soft/grainy/coarse.
- A lot of sand feels heavy on my hand.
- Sand can be piled up.
- Wet sand can be poked.
- Sand is quiet.
- You can't see through sand.
- Sawdust is fine like sand.
- Rice and beans feel different from sand and they are noisier.

To summarize the experience, note that children enjoy both fine and coarse sand: coarse sand is easier to mold when wet; fine sand works well with sifters and colanders. Point out that teachers sometimes offer children other substances such as rice in place of sand because they provide a different experience and are sometimes easier to clean up. Emphasize that while other materials such as rice or beans are good for pouring, weighing, and measuring, they are not a substitute for sand.

Activity: Using Props to Stimulate Sand and Water Play

Point out that water and sand alone will not maintain children's interest for long. By adding a variety of interesting props, children will continue to explore sand and water, learning many concepts in the process.

Display on a table the props you have collected for the session and allow participants to select the ones they want. Allow 10 to 15 minutes for participants, in small groups, to experiment with the props in sand and water. Ask them to consider the following:

"Which props work best with sand?"

"What do you think children would do with these props?"

"What skills and concepts might they learn using these props with sand and water?"

Keep a running list of responses to the last question.

Assignment:

Ask participants to try out a new sand or water activity in the classroom, adding props they haven't used before. Observe how children use the materials and what they say and learn. See the *Creative Curriculum* for ideas on props.

Exploring Math and Science Concepts with Sand and Water

> **Participants in this workshop will:**
>
> • identify some of the many math and science concepts that children learn through sand and water play; and
>
> • develop strategies for expanding children's experiences with sand and water.

Materials needed:

- Chart pad and markers

- Water table and/or individual plastic tubs

- Sand table and/or individual plastic tubs

- Props for sand and water including those from session #1 plus small cars and trucks, twigs, heavy cardboard, small cardboard boxes, leaves; five objects that will float, five that will sink; cotton, blotters, sponges, small lightweight blocks of wood; paper towels

- *The Creative Curriculum* videotape and VCR

Discussion: What Is Science?

Explain that as children play with sand and water, they discover many math and science concepts. In the *Creative Curriculum* an important part of the teacher's role is to provide the props children need to make such discoveries and to extend their learning experiences.

Ask participants to think about what scientists do. For example, scientists:

- find out how things work
- think up new ways to do things
- discover through trial and error
- compare things
- observe how things change
- ask "what would happen if?"
- experiment
- explore
- solve problems
- use special equipment such as a microscope, telescope, magnifying glass, and test tubes

Next, select a few of the responses and ask participants to give examples of children being scientists. For example:

- A scientist finds out how things work: Children discover how sand and water can make a wheel turn.

- A scientist observes changes: Children observe what happens when you add water to sand.

Summarize the discussion by pointing out that children discover many science concepts as they play with sand and water.

Activity: Math and Science Concepts in Sand and Water Play

List the following math and science concepts on the chart pad:

MATH	SCIENCE
Measurements—how many? Volume—how much? Weight—how heavy? Classification—what goes together? Seriation—large to small/tall to short Conservation—how things stay the same	How properties change What holds water/what dissolves in water? What floats/sinks? How do things look under the magnifying glass? Which objects freeze/melt?

Form groups of three or four. Have each group select a different math or science concept and complete the following assignment:

- Design an activity using sand and water to help children discover the concept you selected.

- Outline the following:

  props you would provide;

  how you would set things up; and

  what you might say to the children as they use the materials.

Allow about 20 minutes for the activity. Give each group a chance to share its activities with the entire group. In summarizing the activity, offer the following suggestions:

- Children will discover many concepts on their own when you provide the props they need. For instance, setting out objects that float or sink will naturally lead to many discoveries about weight and buoyancy.

- Children may need help to verbalize the concepts they are discovering.

- When talking with children, teachers should first ask them to describe what they are doing. For children who are reluctant to express themselves, teachers can ask questions such as these:

  "How does it sound?"
  "Do they look the same?"
  "What would happen if...?"
  "How much do you think will fit...?"
  "What else could you...?"
  "Do you know what this is called?"

- By asking open-ended questions such as the ones given below, teachers can further encourage children to describe what they are doing and to think about what else they might do.

  "Tell me about what you made."

  "Why do think the mud pies don't hold their shape?"

  "You really made the water wheel go fast. How could you make it turn slowly?"

  "I see you're trying to pour the sand into that little opening. What could you use to get the sand in the bottle without spilling it?"

  "What could we use these shells for in the sand tub?"

Activity: Extending Children's Play with Sand and Water

Reiterate that an important part of the teacher's role is to extend children's learning by providing new experiences to stimulate growth and development. One way to do this with sand and water is to create a specific experiment or experience for the children.

Form groups of four or five and assign each group one of the following tasks:

1. Create a dramatic play scene for the sand table. (Provide small cardboard boxes, twigs, seashells, plastic animals, small trucks and cars, pipe cleaners, popsicle sticks, etc.)

2. Create a variety of bubble blowers. (Provide pipe cleaners, straws, funnels, wooden strips, toothpicks, bubble pipes, plastic berry baskets, and bubble soap.) How many different sizes and shapes of bubbles can you make with your blowers?

3. Think of a variety of weighing activities. (Provide either a ready-made scale or a homemade balance scale with various types of containers for sand and water, such as styrofoam cups, margarine containers, paper plates, or yogurt containers.)

Allow at least 20 to 30 minutes for this activity. Have each group share what it has made and demonstrate how its creations work.

Summarize the exercise and end the workshop by emphasizing that teachers can extend children's sand and water play activities through ongoing reinforcement of their efforts. For those children who appear to be stuck at a particular level or for those who are reluctant to participate in sand and water activities, it is very important that teachers know when and how to intervene. Intervention is not interference; rather, it is a natural extension of learning, rooted in observation and reinforcement. As used in the *Creative Curriculum*, intervention in the sand and water area means:

- starting with basic props and observing children's play to see when new props are needed (e.g., when children are experimenting with how to fill a bottle, a funnel can be introduced);

- presenting materials to children sequentially (e.g., first dry sand and then wet; first clear water and later colored water or soapy water); and

- providing raw materials children may need for experiments:

    different surfaces they can pour water on, such as wax paper, a blotter, a sponge, or plastic;

    objects that will sink or float;

    a series of cans with holes punched in them so children can see how long it takes for the different cans to empty; and/or

    materials that are proportional, such as measuring or nesting cups.

Using strategies such as these, the teacher creates an environment in which children are encouraged to experiment on their own. The child still takes the lead in learning; the teacher's role is to ensure that learning takes place.

Videotape: *The Creative Curriculum*

To conclude the workshop, show the portion of the videotape on sand and water. Ask participants to particularly note how teachers promote learning and problem solving.

VIII. Library Workshops

The goal of these workshops is to impart the value of the library corner as a distinct and exciting interest area. The underlying theme in each suggested workshop is that the library area is more than just a bookshelf and a place to read stories; it is an interest area that offers children a wide variety of experiences that promote literacy.

Through small group activities and discussions, participants explore ways to bring literature alive for young children and to convey a love for books and stories that stimulate their imagination and enhance self-expression.

Workshop	Page
Reading to Young Children	146
Selecting Books for Young Children	150
Extending Literature through Creative Activities	153

Reading to Young Children

> **Participants in this workshop will:**
>
> • explore specific techniques for reading to young children;
>
> • discuss when and where to read to young children; and
>
> • identify the benefits of exposing children to books and stories.

Materials needed:

• Chart pad, markers, and tape

• A selection of books such as the following:

The Very Hungry Caterpillar by Eric Carle,
Noisy Nora by Rosemary Wells
Gilberto and the Wind by Marie Etts
Madeline by Ludwig Bemmelmans
Curious George by H. A. Reg
The Snowy Day by Ezra J. Keats
Moving Day by Tobi Tobias, and
Stone Soup by Marsha Brown

• An adult-size chair and child-size chair

• *The Creative Curriculum* videotape and VCR

Group Activity: Techniques for Reading to Young Children

Ask for five volunteers to sit on the floor and pretend they are young children listening to a story. Ask the rest of the group to observe how you read the story. Begin by reading the story *Madeline* by Ludwig Bemmelmans. Sit on an adult-size chair and begin without introducing the book. Hold the book so that the illustrations are only partially visible. Do not include the group in telling the story. Stop after reading several pages and move to the smaller chair. Hold the book so that everyone can see the illustrations, and involve the participants in telling the story. Finish the book.

Lead the group in a discussion of the two approaches you just demonstrated. Have participants identify appropriate ways to read stories. Emphasize the following guidelines:

• Sit on a low chair so you are closer to the children.

• Hold the book to one side so the children can see the pictures as the story is read.

• Speak clearly to suit the story, varying the tempo.

• Be dramatic—your voice should change for different characters.

- If some children are having difficulty listening, ask questions to get their attention. ("What do you think will happen next?")

- Invite children to join in whenever possible with refrains and responses.

Next, ask participants to form groups of three and give each group one of the books listed under "Materials Needed" for this session. Ask each group to discuss:

- "When would be an appropriate time to read this book?"

- "How would you introduce this book?"

- "How could you involve the children in telling this story?"

Allow about 10 to 15 minutes for this task. As each group reports, you may want to emphasize the following points:

- Always be familiar with a story before sharing it with children. Reviewing the book ahead of time will provide answers to important questions such as the following:

    How long will it take to read the book, and can the children sit still for that length of time?

    Are there places where the children can join in (for example, repeated phrases, questions posed in the book)?

    Is there anything special about the illustrations that the children might notice (for example, tiny details, hidden surprises)?

    Are sound effects part of the story, and how can they enhance the experience (animal noises, sirens, etc.)?

- Design an approach to gaining the children's interest. Children will be more likely to listen to a story if they have a reason to be interested. One way to do this is to tie the theme of the book to something the children have recently experienced:

    the birth of a sibling;
    the first snowfall;
    a visit or field trip;
    a child who is moving; or
    a discovery made by the children.

- Refer participants to the book lists in the *Creative Curriculum*. Note that these books describe typical situations and characters who face issues that children can easily identify with. Explain that the list is a sampling, and both teachers and parents should select books that address the needs, feelings, and experiences of the children in their care.

- Show the children the cover of the book or the first illustration and ask questions to gain their attention.

    "What do you see happening in this picture?"

"Why do you think this boy looks so happy?"

- Bring in an object that is an important part of the book and talk about it.

  "Here's a nice round stone I found on the playground. Do you think we could make soup from this stone? Let's see what happens in this book called *Stone Soup*."

Discussion: The Value of Sharing Books with Children

Ask participants to think about what they enjoy about reading books as adults, and what they remember enjoying about reading books when they were children. Allow a few minutes for the group to think, and record their responses on the chart pad. You may hear:

- "It's relaxing to read a novel."

- "I learn a lot from books."

- "I can escape to another place through books."

Point out that studies show that one of the most effective ways to encourage young children to want to become readers is to read to them every day. Looking at books and listening to stories opens up many new opportunities and experiences for young children, including the following:

- Children expand their imaginations and creativity.

- Children learn to deal with life experiences (e.g., birth of a sibling, moving, illness, etc.).

- Children come to understand that their feelings, fears, and problems are not unique to them.

- Children learn about social responsibilities, such as how to be a good friend, how to share and take turns, and how to behave in specific social situations.

- Children learn new ideas, such as what other people and places are like.

By carefully selecting books that reflect the children's life experiences, interests, and developmental capabilities and by sharing them in a supportive and comfortable setting, teachers can help children learn to love books as they develop the skills they need to read. When teachers themselves recognize the value of reading, they are better able to convey a love of books to young children.

Next, ask participants when and where they read to children in the classroom. Emphasize the following points:

- Children enjoy hearing a story as a group and in small groups, but they also enjoy reading alone with a teacher.

- Reading stories can be part of circle time, free play in the library corner, before nap, at the end of the day, and so forth.

Videotape: *The Creative Curriculum*

Show the portion of the videotape on the library corner. Have participants note how teachers promote an interest in books and writing. The following scenes are shown:

- a teacher reading to one child;

- a child helping to read the story;

- a group experience being recorded; and

- how a teacher handles a situation where children are becoming restless during a story.

Assignment:

Ask participants to bring two of their favorite children's books to the next session.

Selecting Books for Young Children

Participants in this workshop will:

- develop criteria for selecting children's books; and

- create a card file of recommended books for young children.

Materials needed:

- Chart pad, markers, and tape

- Seven 3 x 5 index cards per participant

- A selection of books, such as the following:

  Bread and Jam for Frances by Russell Hoban
  Teeny Tiny by Tomie de Pablo
  Swimming by Leo Linnai
  Corduroy by Dan Freeman
  Ira Sleeps Over by Bernard Waber
  My Doctor by Harlow Rockwell
  Will I Have a Friend? by Miriam Cohen
  Blueberries for Sal by Robert McCloskey
  Make Way for Ducklings by Robert McCloskey

Activity: Developing Criteria for Selecting Children's Books

Form groups of four or five and ask each group to select a recorder who will report on the discussion. Give each group two of the books you brought to this session and have them add their own favorite books. Ask them to sort out which books are appropriate for preschoolers (threes and early fours) and which are appropriate for older fours and fives. Put the following question for groups to consider in reviewing their books:

- What would children like about this book?

- Would it appeal equally to boys and girls? Why or why not?

- Would children like the illustrations? Why or why not?

- Is the book appropriate for your group of children? Why or why not?

Allow 20 to 30 minutes for this activity, then invite the reporters to share the highlights of their group's discussion. As each group reports, list the criteria that emerges for selecting children's books. Emphasize that knowing how to select books is especially important because there are so many available that are not appropriate. For young preschoolers, note that they particularly like stories:

- centered on themselves, their families, their homes, and their friends;

- about characters they can identify with;

- with lots of repetition in the story so they can join in;

- with engaging language, rhymes, and nonsense words; and

- with colorful and bold illustrations that are clear, realistic, and filled with detail. However, when evaluating illustrations, color is not the sole criteria; many wonderful illustrations are black-and-white line drawings or graphics.

Four- and five-year-olds tend to enjoy books with more of a story. They can sit for a longer period of time and appreciate a story with humor or imagination. Books that are appropriate for this age group have the following characteristics:

- a plot they can follow;

- a story with humor or perhaps a surprise ending;

- imaginative stories about things that young children *know* couldn't happen; and

- stories that extend their understanding of the world around them.

Books for young children should be non-discriminatory and inclusive of our rich diversity as people. Ask participants what would they look for to ensure that the books they choose meet this criteria. Emphasize the following points:

- Stories should feature men and women in a variety of roles displaying the ability to make decisions, solve problems, display a wide range of emotions, care for family members, and work outside the home.

- Family groupings should reflect different kinds of families (e.g., single parent families, families with a mother and father, families with two mothers and two fathers, interracial families, two children and a grandmother, etc.).

- Illustrations should portray people realistically—for example, mothers who wear clothing other than aprons—and reflect diversity, including people with disabilities, of different ages, and a variety of ethnic backgrounds.

Activity: Creating a Card File

A card file helps teachers find the books they need when they need them. As new interests and needs emerge or the children make new discoveries and experience new things, teachers can use the file to locate appropriate books. For example, if the children are talking about dinosaurs, or if a particular child is going to the hospital, books on these topics can be provided.

Ask the participants to think of all the themes they could use to classify books in a card file and list them on the chart pad. The list may include the following:

- Feelings
- Seasons
- Pets
- Community workers
- Colors
- Birthdays
- School

Encourage participants to create a classification system that works best for them, and note that the same book can be cross-classified by more than one theme. Some teachers may want to categorize books by their favorite author as well.

Provide each participant with seven 3 x 5 index cards. Ask them to select seven books from those available (books you have provided and the ones participants brought to share) to begin their card file. Be sure each card includes:

- title,
- author(s),
- one- or two- sentence summary of the book, and
- category/theme.

Allow 15 to 20 minutes for the activity. End the session by encouraging participants to update their card files and share the ideas with another teacher in their program.

Assignment:

Ask teachers to use their local library to select five books from the list in the *Creative Curriculum* and bring them to the next session.

Extending Literature through Creative Activities

Participants in this workshop will:

- discover new ways to use books and stories to expand children's creativity and imagination; and

- explore the value of storytelling.

Materials needed:

- Chart pad, markers, and tapes

- The following books (plus those participants will bring):

  Peter's Chair by Ezra Keats

  Stone Soup by Marcia Brown

  Where the Wild Things Are by Maurice Sendak

  Caps for Sale by Esphyr Slobodkina

  Alexander and the Terrible, Horrible, No Good, Very Bad Day by Judith Viorst

  A Birthday for Frances by Russell Hoban

- Record: "Where the Wild Things Are"

Activity: Extending Stories through Music and Dramatic Play

Read the story *Where the Wild Things Are* by Maurice Sendak and invite participants to use their bodies to represent the movement/actions of the wild things, as you would with children.

- "How do you think wild things dance?"

- "Show me your terrible claws."

- "What do wild things do when they are tired?"

You can provide background music for these movement activities such as the "Where the Wild Things Are" record, or a similar recording or song.

Next, form small groups and ask each group to select a book from those they have brought and describe how they could extend the children's learning with that book. Allow 15 to 20 minutes for the activity. Ask each group to demonstrate its ideas. In summarizing, you might offer the following suggestions:

- Read *Stone Soup* by Marcia Brown and have the children make stone soup as a cooking experience.

- Read *Caps for Sale* by Esphyr Slobodkina at the park and have the children climb the jungle gym and pretend to be the monkeys as you reread the story.

• Read *Moving Day* by Tobi Tobias and convert your house corner into a moving van.

Discussion: Using Questions to Extend Stories

Explain that another way to extend stories is to ask open-ended questions that encourage children to share their own experiences. Here are some examples.

• *Alexander and the Terrible, Horrible, No Good, Very Bad Day:*

> "Have you ever felt like Alexander did? What was your terrible, horrible, no good, very bad day?"

• *A Birthday for Frances:*

> "It was really hard for Frances when it was Gloria's birthday. How do you feel when your sisters or brothers have a birthday?"

• *Peter's Chair:*

> "Did your mother ever give something of yours to your sister or brother? How did that make you feel?"

Here participants look at one of the books they brought and think of several questions they could ask to encourage children to think about the story.

Discussion: Storytelling

Some people have a gift for telling stories. (If you know someone or find that one of the participants likes to tell stories, plan ahead to have this person share a story with the group.) Storytelling opens up a new world of literature for many children, especially those who need more eye-to-eye contact and a more animated style to keep their attention.

Encouraging children to tell stories themselves builds important skills for reading. When children are encouraged to tell stories, their language tends to be animated and expressive. They use details to describe a long series of things that happen to a particular character in their story. They often begin with "once upon a time," specify a place and time where the action takes place, describe one or more characters, and include a sequence of events.

There are many questions teachers can ask to encourage a child to tell a story.

• "Who is in your story?"
• "Where is this person?"
• "What happened first?"
• "Then what happened?"
• "How did he react to that?"
• "What happened at the end?"

A storytelling game can involve the whole group. The story starts and then someone points to the next person to continue. You can demonstrate this to conclude the workshop.

> "It was a cold, dark night. I was walking home from the store when I heard a strange noise behind me. It sounded like..."

IX.   Music and Movement Workshops

Music and movement bring a special dimension to the early childhood classroom, from providing opportunities for children to develop muscle coordination to strategies for changing the "mood" of the room and helping children (and adults!) relax.

This series of workshops can help teachers—even those teachers who declare that they are **not** musically inclined—to feel more comfortable about introducing singing, percussion, and other kinds of music-making, movement, and dance activities to young children. The workshops outline the socio-emotional, cognitive, and physical skills and concepts that children learn and practice as they engage in music and movement activities. Participants will share experiences including music and movement in their program, and teach each other favorite songs and games. They will have an opportunity to make instruments and learn about creative movement activities for group settings.

Workshops: **Page**

  The Importance of Music and Movement... 156

  Making Music.. 164

  Movement Activities 168

Handouts:

  "What Children Are Learning" (Handout #1)... 160

  "Favorite Songs" (Handout #2) 163

  "Different Ways to Move" (Handout #3)... 170

The Importance of Music and Movement

Participants in this workshop will:

- explore how music affects all of us;

- identify how music activities promote children's socio-emotional, cognitive, and physical development; and

- describe ways that adults can facilitate children's participation in music activities.

Materials needed:

- Chart pad, markers, and tape

- Tape player

- Cassette tapes of a variety of types of music, such as children's songs and folk music, children's exercise and movement music, music from the cultures represented by the participants as well as from other cultures, quiet music (lullabies), classical music, jazz, rock, opera, and current "hits"

Handouts:

- "What Children Are Learning" (Handout #1)

- "Favorite Songs" (Handout #2)

Activity: Music in Our Lives

Play lively music as participants enter the room. Replace this with quieter, slower music as you begin the session. Ask participants to describe how they felt when they entered the room and heard the lively music. What did they think this workshop would be like, based on what they were hearing? Did they think something different when the music changed? Why?

Share your own views on the role music has played in your life. For example, talk about when you listen to music, what kinds you like, and so on. Invite participants to share their views.

Discuss how playing favorite musical selections and singing together can build a sense of community in a classroom and make everyone feel a part of the group. Music and movement can help set the tone and determine the mood of the classroom. Lively music and fast movement help children to increase their activity level; quiet, slower music brings the level down. Children may be more motivated to engage in less active experiences, such as reading and preparing to rest, when the music is quieter. Slower movement activities can lead children to concentrate on how their bodies move, what each muscle can do, and how their muscles feel when they are at rest.

Activity: Getting through the Day with Music

There are many different ways in which children engage in music and movement activities. How they do so depends a lot on their stage of development, the role of music in their family life, and in their community, and their previous experiences with singing, playing instruments, and dancing. Discuss the types of music and movement activities featured in the *Creative Curriculum* as outlined below:

- **Listening**—children's musical attention generally increases with age, as well as their ability to notice variations in musical selections (changes in tempo, rhythm, volume, pitch); most older children can listen to their own singing or playing to match or correct tones.

- **Singing**—at first, most children can sing along with others but not always in time or in tune; later they can match tones as they sing with others, sing alone, and sing in tune.

- **Movement to music**—young children will often move to their own beat rather than the beat of live or recorded music; by three or four years of age they should be able to "keep time" to a regular beat and, with practice, create different movements according to the music that is playing; while most preschoolers can dance to music, "directed" or "learned" dances are more appropriate for older children.

- **Playing instruments**—young children first manipulate and experiment with instruments, and later become aware of differences in sounds of various instruments. With practice, children will use instruments to accompany their movements or singing, increasingly coordinating their playing with the rhythm.

Ask participants to name some of the songs they like to use with young children. For example, ask them what songs they use to start the day and build a sense of community. Record their song titles on a chart pad. You might add your own favorites to the list (such as "Hello") or songs you've made up (for example, "This is the Way We Start Our Day, Start Our Day, Start Our Day..."). If you have a cassette tape with any of your favorite songs, play it and invite the group to sing along.

Ask participants how they would introduce a new song like the ones they just sang to a group of children. Record their responses on a chart pad. Try to bring out the following ideas.

- Gather the group together by singing a song (e.g., "The More We Get Together").

- Begin with something meaningful for children, such as a song that includes their names (e.g., "Hello" or "Friends, Friends, 1,2,3").

- Use songs or chants with a consistent melody and lots of repetition in the text.

- Select songs that are lively and quick more often than slow ones; use songs that are funny or nonsensical.

- Try singing or chanting directions to children, such as, "Let's all clean up, let's all clean up, let's all clean up the room."

- Reinforce the fun of singing by making a tape of the children singing—alone, all together, with you.

- Sing the same song in different ways—loudly, softly, quickly, slowly, with different tempos (rock, polka, cha-cha, waltz, etc.).

- Use a higher range of your singing voice—young children's natural singing voices are closest to that of a female soprano.

- Begin by singing or playing a song for the children; ask them to tell you what they heard (which will give you an idea about what you'll need to focus on as you continue to teach the song to them).

- After the first time you sing a sing with the children, begin to leave out words or phrases for the children to fill in (begin with the repeated or the rhyming words).

Discuss some of the ways teachers can use songs during the day and the various types of songs. For example:

- Songs to help children learn each other's names

- Songs to ease transitions

- Songs to make everyone feel better

- Songs that describe children's actions

- Songs that build on a theme in a story you've just read, or a recent field trip

Have participants work in small groups to identify songs for each category. If the group seems comfortable with the idea, ask each small group to perform one of their songs for the rest of the participants.

Activity: What Children Learn from Music and Movement

Lead a discussion of how music and movement activities are used in the classroom. What skills and concepts can children acquire and enhance as they sing, engage in creative movement activities, march, and dance? Record ideas that are shared on the chart pad.

Distribute Handout #1, "What Children Are Learning," and have participants form groups of four. Explain that this is a two-part task. First, each group will identify music and movement activities that promote children's growth and development in each of the learning objectives listed in the left column. (Note: The skills and concepts listed on the handout are taken from the *Creative Curriculum* Child Development and Learning Checklist.)

When each group has completed this task, invite participants to share the activities they listed. Note how a variety of music and movement activities can help achieve the same objectives.

The second part of the task is to discuss the role of the teacher in facilitating children's learning through music and movement activities. Ask participants to think about the following questions as they consider each activity they listed:

- How would you arrange the environment for this activity?
- For what time of day would you plan the activity?
- What materials would you need for the activity?
- What would your interactions with children during this activity include?

The completed charts might look likes the one

Developmental Area & Objectives	Music/Movement Activity	Teacher's Role in Activity
Socio-emotional development *Demonstrates confidence in growing abilities*	Beats drum in time to music	Play tape during circle time; distribute musical instruments to children; encourage a shy child to play the drum: tell a child, "Listen to the sound you're making with that drum! It's a big sound."
Participates in routines easily	Joins morning circle time	Lead children in a song that prepares them to end free play, put away the materials they were using, and sit in the circle area
Physical development *Shows balance in use of large muscles*	Participates in "stationary" movement activities	Lead children in circle time activity: "Twist like a pretzel...twinkle like a star"
Demonstrates skills in discriminating sounds	Listens to music and talks about how it sounds	In the listening center, play portions of several pieces of music (classical, country, jazz, opera, etc.); ask children to tell you about the music they're hearing—how does it sound, how does it make them feel, and so on
Cognitive development *Shows curiosity and desire to learn*	Tries new endings to familiar songs	Sing several songs with children throughout the week; note when children are comfortable with the music and words; sing softly with several children in the listening center, asking them to help you make up new endings
Makes believe with objects	Uses scarves and other props for creative movement	Take tape player and several cassette tapes, scarves, streamers, hoops, capes, and other props outdoors; play music; ask children to "move to the music"

Handout #1: What Children Are Learning

Review the developmental objectives listed in the left column. With other members of your group, think of music and movement activities that you could plan and conduct to promote children's growth in each developmental area. Record specific singing, percussion, movement, and dance activities in the space in the middle column. Describe the role of the teacher in facilitating the activity.

Developmental Area/Objective	Music/Movement Activity	Teacher's Role in Activity
Socio-emotional development *Demonstrates confidence in growing abilities*		
Demonstrates interest and participates in class activities		
Participates in routine activities easily		
Works cooperatively with others		
Physical development *Runs with control over direction and speed*		
Shows balance in use of large muscles		

Developmental Area/Objective	Music/Movement Activity	Teacher's Role in Activity
Coordinates eye and hand movements		
Demonstrates skills in discriminating sounds		
Cognitive development *Shows curiosity and desire to learn*		
Finds more than one solution to a problem		
Recalls the sequence of events		
Recognizes patterns and can repeat them		
Takes on a pretend role		
Recalls words in a song or a play		

Assignment:

Conclude the workshop by giving out a list of materials participants will need to bring to the next workshop if they want to make a musical instrument. (See materials list for the next workshop.)

Distribute Handout #2, "Favorite Songs," that identifies five different types of songs and asks participants to list their favorite songs in each category. (There is also a space for an additional category.) Invite them to bring favorite tapes or records to the next workshop and to share some of their most successful songs with the group.

As participants prepare to leave, play appropriate "recessional" music (such as a march from an opera).

Handout #2: Favorite Songs

Types of Songs	Favorites
Songs with repetition	
Finger plays	
Singing games	
Songs for transitions	
Songs from different cultures	
Other types of songs	

Making Music

> **Participants in this workshop will:**
>
> • share and learn about different types of songs that appeal to young children;
>
> • use musical instruments in a variety of ways; and
>
> • make musical instruments they can share with children.

Materials needed:

- Chart pad and markers

- Tape player or record player

- Cassette tapes or records of a variety of types of music, including music for singing along and music for movement, percussion, and dance activities

- Copies of the section on making musical instruments from the *Creative Curriculum*

- Completed Handout #2 on "Favorite Songs"

- Books that contain rhymes, repetition, and other musical elements (see the list in the Library Module of the *Creative Curriculum*)

- Materials for making musical instruments and samples of completed instruments. (Amounts and lengths listed are sufficient for one or a pair, of each item; you will need more for multiple instruments made by participants.)

  Drums

      large oatmeal box
      40" shoestring
      rubber inner tube
      paint
      scissors

  Drumsticks

      2 dowels (10" to 12")
      2 wooden beads with holes
      glue (nontoxic)
      scissors

  Bell Band

      6" of elastic, 1" wide
      small bells

needle and thread
velcro (optional)

Kazoo

empty toilet paper tube
contact paper or paint and brush
rubber band
scissors
wax paper (2" by 2")

Maraca

several bottle caps
construction paper, colorful contact paper, tin foil, or paint
6 to 10 pieces of 12" ribbon or paper (1/2" wide)
paper towel roll
piece of lightweight cardboard
tape

Sand Blocks

2 small boxes with tops (2" by 2" by 4")
2 pieces of elastic (6" long, 1/2" wide)
paint, construction paper, tin foil, or colorful contact paper
6" by 6" piece of sandpaper
measuring tape or string
tape
scissors
thread and needle
paste or household cement
ruler

Shaker

empty oatmeal box
clothespin (nonclipping type)
small plastic medicine bottle cap (1" to 2" in diameter)
bells or buttons
scissors
glue or paste (nontoxic)
tape
paint (nontoxic)
paintbrush
12" by 12" piece of construction paper, colorful cloth, or contact paper

Activity: Singing with Children

Begin the workshop with a song that everyone knows or one you want to introduce to the group.

On the chart pad, list the types of songs that appeal to young children (Handout #2). Briefly review what children like about each type of song and refer participants to the discussion in the *Creative Curriculum.* Invite participants to share their favorite songs in each category, teaching them to the group. In this way, everyone will have augmented their repertoire of songs to use with children.

Invite participants to talk about the ways that they have used these songs with the children in their group. What did they do that helped to make the singing activities successful? Were there any problems? How did they solve them?

Conclude this part of the workshop by asking participants to discuss the times of the day that they use singing with the children. How/when do they use songs on records and tapes? When do they invent their own songs (e.g., during clean up)? What are some examples of invented songs? Ask a participant to make up a transition song to lead the group to the next workshop activity, "Making Music."

Activity: Making Music

Introduce this activity by noting that there are many ways that we can "make music" with children. We can help children notice sounds that naturally occur around us; appreciate the richness of language; and learn to use musical instruments.

Ask the group to sit silently for a minute and concentrate on the sounds in and outside the room.

- What types of sounds do they hear?
- What might be making these sounds?
- Which sounds are pleasant? Why?
- Which sounds are not pleasant? Why?
- Which sounds have a pattern or rhythm? Can you repeat the pattern with your voice, hands, or feet?

Talk about the sounds that we hear throughout the day, every day. How do they enrich our lives? How can we help children to notice the variety of sounds that are around us all the time?

Next, note the language itself, made up of sounds and rhythms, share many of the qualities of music. Read to participants (or ask them to read) excerpts from children's poetry and books that are full of rhymes, repetition, and other musical sounds (see list in the Library section of the *Creative Curriculum* for suggested titles).

Next, lead a discussion on musical instruments. Talk about the instruments that you have heard played (and/or that you play yourself). Ask participants to share experiences they have had listening to/playing instruments. What made them enjoyable experiences? How can teachers help children enjoy listening to and playing musical instruments?

Distribute the instruments you have brought. Ask participants to again listen for patterns of sounds and rhythms in/outside the room. Then, ask participants to repeat the sounds individually, in pairs, in trios, as a full orchestra. Have participants sound out their names with the instruments. How could they use these activities with the children in their group?

Summarize by discussing ways to introduce instruments into the classroom.

- Give children beating sticks to accompany the rhythm of their names, to use while they listen to music, later to accompany their movement activities.

- Tell children the names of instruments as you distribute them, how to care for and handle instruments properly.

- Give younger children a limited choice of instruments from which to select.

- Help children to begin and end with recorded music (or music you are playing on the piano or autoharp) that they are accompanying.

- Allow children to explore music with instruments during free play.

- Ask several children to accompany the dancing of others with musical instruments.

Activity: Making Musical Instruments

Materials for making instruments should be set out on tables with the directions from the *Creative Curriculum*. If you feel it would be helpful, you may want to demonstrate the process for making each of the instruments, or you can serve as a resource as participants begin their work. (Try making each of the instruments yourself before this workshop, so you can anticipate some of the problems and know how to resolve them.)

Conclude this session by leading participants in singing and accompanying recorded music with the instruments they have made.

Movement Activities

Participants in this workshop will:

• practice a variety of movement activities appropriate for young children;

• discuss how these activities enhance children's development.

Materials needed

• Chart pad, markers, and tape

• Tape player

• Cassette tapes of a variety of types of music

• Props for movement activities, such as scarves and streamers, hoops, capes, wrist-bells, maracas, other instruments

Handout

• "Different Ways to Move" (Handout #3)

Discussion: Children's Development and Movement Activities

Play lively music as participants enter the room. As you begin the session, play softer music and help the participants to relax and focus by leading them in a song that brings the group together such as "Hello."

Review with participants the developmental milestones for three- to five-year-old children that were addressed in the first workshop, focusing on the ways that children move. The discussion should include the following capabilities of young children:

• Demonstrates confidence in their growing abilities

• Enjoys participating in movement activities

• Recalls the sequence of events

• Recognizes patterns and can repeat them

• Runs with control over direction and speed

• Shows balance in use of large muscles

• Demonstrates skill in discriminating sounds

Ask participants to identify movement activities that use these and other skills. Record their responses on a chart pad. The activities might include:

- Going from one place in the room (or outdoors) to another, using a variety of ways to move

- Moving one's body in various ways, without moving from one place to another

- Pantomiming activities with one's body (such as pretending to move imaginary things, moving like elephants or other animals, acting out the ways that characters in a book are moving)

- Matching movement to music

Tell participants that they will have an opportunity to try out these and other movements. First, they should think about ways that they could introduce movement activities to children. Ask participants to list these as you record them on a chart pad. Try to emphasize the following ideas:

- Observe how children naturally move throughout the day and plan activities around those movements; point out to children what they are doing: "I see Cassie moving her arms, hips, and legs!"

- Join in when children are dancing; follow their lead, then add a variation.

- Introduce simple activities that involve children walking from one place to another (indoors and outdoors); tell the children what your START and STOP signal is (clapping your hands, banging a drum, ringing a bell); ask them to walk slow/fast, high/low, as if they are happy/sad/angry.

- Add to the walking activities by asking children to move from one place to another in different ways.

Activity: Exploring Different Ways to Move

Distribute Handout #3. Divide the participants into four small groups and assign each group one section of the handout to complete. Ask each group to identify several movement activities in the category assigned and to try the movements themselves. Give group #4 the props, tape recorder, and cassette tapes.

After the participants have completed their section of the handout, ask each group to lead the other participants in the movement activities they identified.

Conclude the session with group #4 leading the participants in moving to music.

Handout #3: Different Ways to Move

Directions: Review the example activities for the category of movement that your group was assigned. Identify other activities for this category and record them in the space provided. Then, practice these movements with your group:

1. What are all the ways you can move from one place to another?

- Taking giant steps

- Walking sideways

- Moving like a heavy animal

- Moving like you're as light as a feather

- _____

- _____

- _____

- _____

- _____

- _____

2. What are all the ways that you can move your body without moving your feet?

- Stretch really high

- Slowly unfold from a seed to a tree

- Twist like a pretzel

- _____

- _____

- _____

- _____

- _____

- _____

3. What are all the ways that you can pantomime movements?

- Lift a hippopotamus

- Lift a feather and ask others, "What am I doing?"

- Move like an elephant and ask others, "What animal am I?"

- Move the way a character in a book moves, then describe the action

- _____

- _____

- _____

- _____

- _____

- _____

4. What are the ways you can move your body to match the music being played?

- Move in a happy way to light, lively music

- Move in a serious way to somber music

- Move with deliberate steps to marching music

- _____

- _____

- _____

- _____

- _____

- _____

X. Cooking Workshops

Cooking activities are an exciting addition to every preschool and kindergarten classroom. The focus of this series of workshops is on conveying the importance of cooking as a learning area that promotes children's total development. Specific guidance is given on using cooking to promote mathematical and scientific thinking. Participants will also learn how to plan cooking activities in their classrooms even when they do not have a separate cooking center.

Workshops: **Page**

    The Importance of Cooking 173

    Learning Math and Science through Cooking 177

    Cooking to Go 181

Handouts:

    "Waldorf Salad" (Handout #1)... 175

    "Learning Through Cooking" (Handout #2) 176

    "Big Bread Baking Project" (Handout #3) 179

    "Cooking on the Go" (Handout #4)...................................... 184

The Importance of Cooking

Participants in this workshop will:

- identify the value of cooking in the classroom; and

- give examples of how cooking enhances all areas of children's growth.

Materials needed:

- Chart pad, markers, and tape

- Ingredients for recipe (sufficient quantities for the number of participants in attendance): apples, celery, raisins, walnuts, mayonnaise

- Equipment for recipe (each participant should have access to equipment): cutting board, mixing bowl, serrated plastic knives, nutcracker, wooden spoons

- Workspace at tables

Handouts:

- "Waldorf Salad" (Handout #1)

- "Learning through Cooking" (Handout #2)

Activity: Exploring   Cooking

In preparation for this activity, make sure that cooking equipment and ingredients are distributed so that participants can do the activity individually, without getting in each other's way.

Explain to participants that they will be doing a cooking activity similar to ones that could take place in the classroom. Like the children, they will be preparing their own snack, using a recipe card.

Advise participants to wash their hands and then begin the cooking activity. When they are finished, they can wash their hands and eat the snack they've prepared while filling in Handout #2. In this handout, they will reflect on their cooking experience and record their findings on the worksheet.

Discussion: The Value of Cooking

Lead participants in summarizing their experience. Some questions you might pose are these:

- "What was the cooking experience like?"

- "How did it make you feel to cook for one rather than for a whole group or a family?"

- "How do you think it would make a child feel to be able to prepare his or her own snack?"

- "Did you have a problem understanding the recipe?"

- "Do you think a child would be able to follow the recipe?"

- "Which part of the activity did you like best?"

- "Were you surprised when you filled out Handout #2 to see how much you had learned while you were cooking?"

Encourage the group to share their responses, concluding with a discussion of Handout #2. Record the group's responses to each category on the chart pad. Responses might include some of the following:

Social Development

- Participate in an activity that's traditionally done by adults

- Develop self-help skills

- Learn to wait for space, equipment, or ingredients

Emotional Development

- Develop a sense of pride in completing a task

- Develop independence—"I did it myself"

- Express creativity

Physical Development

- Refine fine muscle control

- Learn directionality

- Develop eye and hand coordination

Cognitive Development

- Learn to "read" a recipe

- Follow a sequence of steps

- Develop mathematical thinking skills by measuring and ordering

Handout #1: Waldorf Salad

1. Cut up 1 apple. Put in mixing bowl.
2. Cut up 1 celery stalk. Put in mixing bowl.
3. Add 10 raisins.
4. Crack 2 walnuts into pieces.
5. Add 1T mayonnaise
6. Mix together. Enjoy!

Handout #2: Learning Through Cooking

Take a few minutes to reflect on the cooking experience you've just completed. Give thought to the ways children learn through an individual cooking experience like the one you've just done. For each of the four areas of development noted below, provide examples of things children might learn during cooking. For example, under cognitive development, you might note that children learn about sequencing when they follow a recipe card. Sequencing is a skill children use in reading and in math.

Social Development:

Emotional Development:

Physical Development:

Cognitive Development:

Learning Math and Science through Cooking

Participants in this workshop will:

- observe firsthand the many math concepts inherent in cooking; and

- observe firsthand the many science concepts inherent in cooking.

Materials needed:

- Chart pad, markers, and tape

- Ingredients for recipe (sufficient quantities for each group of five in attendance): water, molasses, dry yeast, flour, salt, olive oil, cornmeal

- Equipment for recipe (each group should have access to equipment): glass measuring cup, large mixing bowl, measuring spoons, wooden spoon, towel

- Workspace

Handout:

- "Big Bread Baking Project" (Handout #3)

Activity: The Cooking Laboratory

Have participants count off into groups of five. In each group, four of the participants will be actively involved in a group cooking project—making bread. As they cook, these individuals should think of how children would react to what is being done. The fifth person in each group (to be designated by the group members) will serve as the "teacher."

Set each group of five up at a workstation with the ingredients and equipment they need. Depending on the amount of time available for this activity, plus your access to an oven, you may wish to shorten this cooking activity. For example, you might choose to conduct this cooking experience only midway through step 7 of the Big Bread Project just to the point where the bread dough begins to rise. You could bring dough already prepared and ready for the oven to provide first-hand experience with the final steps during the workshop. Or, you could schedule other activities during the time set aside for the dough to rise. The important point is that participants experience the process of cooking—whether or not you continue through to the final product is up to you.

Once you have decided how much of the recipe you will have the group do, distribute Handout #3 to each group of five. Give the following instructions to the "teacher" of each group:

> As you are leading the bread-making activity, point out as many ways as you can to introduce science and math concepts. Some of the things you might want to focus on are these:
>
> - measurement
> - sequencing

- volume
- equivalency
- shape
- size
- physical changes
- chemical changes
- time

Allow sufficient time for the groups to complete the designated steps. After the participants have had time to clean up the workspace and themselves, re-convene the full group.

Discussion: Using Questions as a Teaching Tool

Ask the "teachers" from each group to share their experiences. Was it easy for them to focus the group's attention on math and science concepts? How did they do this? Did they find that the cooking activity lent itself well to this assignment or was it a stretch to tie in math and science? Which concepts were easiest to introduce? Which were hardest?

Then, ask the "cooks" to share their experiences. Were they surprised by how much children could learn during a cooking activity?

Following this, lead the group in brainstorming questions that teachers might use to focus children's attention on math and science concepts. In doing this, remind participants that open-ended questions are usually the best, since they require children to think and reflect upon their responses. As questions are suggested, record them on the chart pad and then discuss how each question attempts to facilitate children's learning of math and science concepts. Here are some sample questions that might be added to the participants' suggestions:

- How can we tell when we have filled the measuring cup with four cups of water? (measurement)

- What step did we do first? What did we do second? Would it have mattered if we did step #1 later on? (sequencing)

- If we know that the dough is going to get bigger when it rests, what size bowl should we put it in? (volume, size)

- How many teaspoons does it take to make one tablespoon? Let's see by filling teaspoons of salt into a tablespoon. (equivalence)

- If we put the dough into a pan shaped liked this (rectangle) to bake, what shape do you think the finished bread will be?

- What happens to the sticky dough when we add flour to it? (physical changes)

- What happens to the water and molasses mixture when we added yeast to it and let it sit? (chemical changes)

Conclude the discussion with the idea that science and math are an integral part of every cooking activity. By helping children to observe and reflect on what they are doing, teachers have a natural way of teaching children these important concepts.

Handout #3:   Big Bread Project

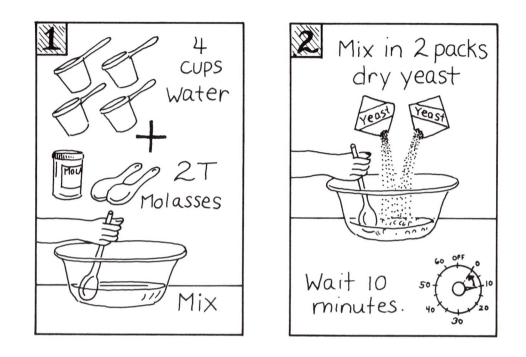

Panel 1: 4 cups water + 2T Molasses Mix

Panel 2: Mix in 2 packs dry yeast Wait 10 minutes.

Panel 3: 12 cups flour Put 5 cups flour in bowl Mix 2½ T salt + 6 cups flour Mix

Panel 4: Put dough on floured work surface Wash bowl

Panel 5: 1 cup flour Sprinkle flour on dough Knead for 15 minutes

6 3 T olive oil

Pour olive oil in bowl

Place dough in bowl

7 Cover bowl with towel

Wait 2 hours
Let dough get
3 X it's size.

8 Put dough back on floured work surface. Knead for 5 minutes.

Shape dough into ball.

Put dough in bowl. Let dough get 2X it's size.

9 Sprinkle cornmeal on a baking sheet.

CORN MEAL

Place dough on sheet.

Cook bread in 375° oven for 45 minutes.

Cooking to Go

Participants in this workshop will:

- explore some of the common barriers to including cooking in the early childhood curriculum;

- develop strategies for being able to creatively respond to the need for doing cooking on a regular basis when obstacles work against this; and

- prepare portable boxes for conducting cooking activities.

Materials needed:

- Sturdy cardboard boxes, preferably with cutouts on sides for carrying

- Equipment for portable boxes:

    plastic mixing bowls
    rolling pin
    rubber spatulas
    wooden spoons
    flour sifter
    cookie cutters
    cookie sheet
    cake pans
    muffin tin
    saucepan with lid
    stock pot
    biscuit cutter
    pastry brush
    pastry bag with several tips and coupler
    pot holders
    trivets
    plastic plates
    plastic flatware
    paper napkins
    toothpicks
    plastic wrap
    aluminum foil
    baker's parchment
    electric wok
    cutting board
    measuring spoons
    measuring cups
    portable electric burner
    can opener
    ladle

- Markers

- Clear contact paper

- Colored construction paper
- Scissors

Handout:

- "Cooking on the Go" (Handout #4)

Discussion: Common Barriers to Cooking

While most teachers are receptive to leading special cooking projects with children, they may not see how they can make cooking an ongoing part of their program. Having discussed the value of cooking in the early childhood curriculum in previous workshops, give participants a chance to brainstorm solutions to common barriers. Begin by asking why teachers are often reluctant to include cooking in their regular program. Record the reasons participants give on a chart pad. Answers may include:

- It's messy
- It's noisy
- It takes up too much of the teacher's time
- It's potentially dangerous
- We don't have the facilities

Once the group has posed a list of problems, lead a discussion of how they might overcome these obstacles. For instance, many cooking activities such as tasting centers can be done without access to a sink or electrical outlets. Supervision and safety might be addressed by scheduling cooking activities during times when volunteers are available to assist. Conclude the discussion by introducing the idea of portable cooking boxes. Refer the group to the section in the *Creative Curriculum* on Creating a Temporary Cooking Area for more information on this idea.

Activity: Making Boxes

Assign each of the four groups the task of making a portable cooking box that could be used by a teacher in setting up a cooking activity. Designate one of the following cooking box assignments to each group:

- Tasting Box

- Baking Box

- Stir-Frying Box

- Soup-Making Box

Alternatively, the groups may come up with their own ideas for box themes.

Allow each group to search through all of the available equipment to put together their box. Encourage participants to assemble their boxes creatively and efficiently. They are free to decorate and label the boxes any way they wish. If more than one box is needed, participants should develop a scheme for labeling what is in each box.

When the groups are finished, they should work together to complete Handout #4. Following this, have each of the groups present their finished portable cooking box to the group.

Assignment:

Have each participant develop a cooking activity that can be used with the portable cooking box their group worked on. In developing the activity, each person should consider:

- whether this is an individual or group activity

- whether children can do this activity independently or if adult supervision is required

- classroom requirements (e.g., access to an outlet, sink, or refrigerator)

- cooking ingredients needed.

Activities, once shared with the group, can be placed in a file folder in the relevant portable box.

Handout #4: Cooking on the Go

Name of "To Go" Box:_____

This portable box can be used for cooking activities such as:

_____

_____

_____

_____

_____

_____

These items are included in this box:

_____

_____

_____

_____

_____

_____

_____

_____

_____

_____

_____

_____

_____

_____

_____

_____

_____

_____

XI. Computer Workshops

Computers are increasingly becoming an important part of early childhood programs. This series of workshops is designed to help teachers who have access to computers to use them in ways that will promote the growth of children socially, emotionally, cognitively and physically. Participants will learn how computers can be used to support children's learning, as well as how to select appropriate software for children.

Workshop   **Page**

The Importance of Computers 186

Critically Evaluating Software 190

Mirroring other Activity Areas.. 193

Handouts:

"Learning through Computers" (Handout #1) 189

"Mirror Planning" (Handout #2) 195

The Importance of Computers

Participants in this workshop will:

- debate the value of computers in the preschool classroom; and

- provide examples of how computers can contribute to all areas of children's learning.

Materials needed:

- Chart pad, markers, and tape

- Computers (as many as possible)

- Developmentally appropriate software such as *The Playroom* or *Electronic Easel*

Handout:

- "Learning through Computers" (Handout #1)

Activity: Debating the Value of Computers

Start off by explaining there is a controversy among experts in early childhood education surrounding the use of computers with young children. Then, write this premise on a chalkboard or chart pad:

> "The introduction of computers in early childhood education, in part to satisfy parental concerns, is a good example of miseducation."
> - David Elkind
> *Miseducation: Preschoolers At Risk,* p. 87

Divide the group in half. One side will be given the task of defending this premise. The other side will be charged with questioning the merits of this premise.

Suggest that each side record its points on chart pad paper. When the teams are done, the responses can be taped to opposing walls. Begin the debate by having each side make a point and then letting the opposing team respond. Some of the points teams are likely to make include these:

Against computers:

- cost
- extra security needed
- require skills too advanced for young children
- they are isolating
- too passive
- children will "burn out"

For computers:

- promotes social development when children work in pairs
- promotes cognitive development by teaching skills, problem solving
- promotes fine motor control through use of keyboard, mouse
- is a good reinforcer of other classroom learning
- helps children make the bridge between concrete and abstract learning
- provides equal access to technology for all children
- are intrinsically motivating for many children

After each side has presented its arguments, lead the full group in a discussion of the pros and cons. As you do this, focus the group's attention on how some of the "cons" might be neutralized through effective planning. For example, if computers are made a part of the regular classroom and children are encouraged to use the computer in pairs, the experience is not an isolating one. Likewise, if software is selected that is open-ended, the child's experience with the computer will be one of active involvement, not passivity. Conclude the activity by referring participants to the section in the *Creative Curriculum* on Why Computers Are Important.

Activity: Exploring What Children Learn Using Computers

In preparation for this activity, assemble as many computers as possible. Assign participants to work at the computers in pairs. If there are not enough computers to go around, have the remaining participants serve as observers and then switch roles so that everyone has a chance to be at the computer. While waiting for a turn, participants might peruse a variety of software programs you have on hand. (For guidance in selecting programs that are developmentally appropriate, consult the listing of Recommended Software and Publishers at the conclusion of the Computers module.)

Direct participants at the computers to go through the program together. They should work out a system for deciding how they will proceed through the program, who will control the mouse, how they will respond to feedback, etc. Those participants who are observing might note what skills a child could develop while engaged in the same tasks.

When everyone has had a turn at the computer, distribute Handout #1. Ask each pair that worked together to complete the Handout as a team. When the teams have finished, lead a group discussion on how computers can promote children's development. To extend the discussion, record responses on a chart pad.

Among the examples participants are likely to come up with are these:

Social Development

- Follow directions

- Plan and execute their plan together

- Learn to share as they work together in pairs

Emotional Development

- Develop pride in doing an adult-like task

- Learn perseverance

Physical Development

- Develop fine motor control by pressing keys

- Improve visual tracking skills by following movement on the screen

- Practice eye-hand coordination by using a mouse to create movement on the screen

Cognitive Development

- Develop reading skills by seeing printed words on the screen

- Experience cause and effect by pushing keys and clicking the mouse

- Learn sequencing by operating computer hardware and software

Conclude with a discussion on how teachers can effectively use computers to support children's learning in exciting, new ways. Refer participants to the section on Making the Decision to Use Computers for further discussion ideas.

Handout #1: Learning through Computers

Take a few minutes to reflect on the computer experience you've just completed. Give thought to the types of learning that children might experience in working at the computer with another child. For each of the four areas of development noted below, provide examples of things children might learn while using a computer. For example, under cognitive development, you might note that children learn about cause and effect when they click on the mouse and something happens on the screen.

Social Development:

Emotional Development:

Physical Development:

Cognitive Development:

Critically Evaluating Software

Participants in this workshop will:

•   develop criteria for selecting developmentally appropriate software;

•   review selected software; and

•   create a classification system for storing software.

Materials needed:

•   Chart pad, markers, and tape

•   Computers (as many as possible)

•   A selection of computer programs that represent both developmentally appropriate and inappropriate software

Discussion: The Software Dilemma

Begin the workshop with a discussion on computer software for young children, focusing the group's attention on why this is such a "hot" topic. In leading the discussion, be sure that these points are covered:

•   Most educational software for children was historically developed by computer experts, not education experts.

•   In an effort to tap into the burgeoning educational market, a great deal of software was produced quickly, without checks for quality control.

•   The great majority of software produced in the early days was of the drill and practice variety, which requires virtually no "child choice."

•   The last five years have seen a dedication to quality. Excellent software that is developmentally appropriate now exists in large quantities.

•   The problem facing early childhood educators today is that truly excellent software co-exists with truly horrible software. Teachers need to be able to weed out the good from the bad so that children are exposed only to appropriate experiences.

Activity: Developing Selection Criteria

Divide the full group into small groups of four or five participants. Give each group several sheets of chart pad paper and some markers. Direct each group to record a set of criteria they would use to select software for young children. If participants need help getting started, consider distributing copies of the "Checklist for Developmentally Appropriate Software" which appears in the section on Selecting Software in the module on Computers.

When the groups have finished, reassemble the full group to learn the results. Among the criteria the groups are likely to designate are these:

- software is appropriate to children's stage of cognitive development (i.e., doesn't require abstract reasoning abilities)

- children can use the program on their own without adult help

- children can move through the program and skip around at will

- the program moves quickly, without any "down" time on the screen

- pictures are used to represent words (e.g., a paintbrush to indicate color, a green light to indicate going to the next activity)

- the program deals with process, rather than a correct answer or a finished product

- different degrees of difficulty can be used

- student progress can be tracked

- a helpful Teacher's Guide accompanies the software

- the content is well defined

- feedback is helpful to the child and nonjudgmental in nature

- representations are bias-free

- content relates to what is going on in other learning centers in the classroom.

As a concluding activity, have the group develop a master checklist that they can use to evaluate software.

Activity: Reviewing Software

In preparation for this activity, assemble 15 to 20 software programs, some of which are developmentally appropriate and some of which are developmentally inappropriate. A simple way to approach this would be to consult a software guide such as *Survey of Early Childhood Software* (Warren Buckleitner, High/Scope Foundation) which lists software of varying quality. Then using the list of publishers contained at the end of the Computers module, either write or phone the publishers and ask for a preview copy. Most publishers will offer preview copies, since software that is well received is likely to be purchased.

Ideally, if there are enough computers, participants can work in pairs reviewing software. If computers are at a premium, divide participants into the appropriate number of groups and let the groups review the software as a team.

Hand out copies of the master checklist and have participants review as many of the software programs as possible. When they have finished, bring the group together to discuss the exercise. Encourage participants to share their feelings about the activity. If any pairs or groups rated software differently, discuss why this happened and how any discrepancies might be resolved.

Activity: Cataloguing Software

Following the review of software, have the participants discuss how they might catalogue the better software so that it can be readily used by children and teachers alike. Some categories for grouping software might include:

- drawing programs

- exploratory programs

- classification and sorting programs

- number and counting programs

- seriation and patterning programs

- science programs (weather, time)

- early reading programs

- early writing programs

- utility programs

Once the categories have been designated, break the full group into small groups. Assign each small group the task of coming up with an icon (picture) to represent one or two of the categories. Picture labels can then be made to place on storage boxes for the disks to make them more accessible.

Mirroring other Activity Areas

Participants in this workshop will:

- discover ways of reinforcing what children are learning in other activity areas of the classroom through computer activities; and

- develop strategies for extending children's learning.

Materials needed:

- Access to classroom with activity areas set up

- Computers (as many as possible)

- Variety of developmentally appropriate software, including these that are specifically designed for mirroring:

  > Building Perspective (Sunburst)
  > Electric Lines (Sunburst)
  > Gertrude's Secrets (The Learning Company)
  > Moptown Hotel (The Learning Company)
  > Moptown Parade (The Learning Company)
  > Puzzle Tanks (Sunburst)

Handout:

- "Mirror Planning" (Handout #2)

Discussion: What Is Mirroring?

Begin this workshop by introducing participants to the instructional technique known as mirroring. Like a mirror reflecting images, the technique of mirroring reflects what is being learned. Mirroring, in fact, is something which naturally goes on in every effective early childhood classroom: a skill or concept is reinforced by presenting it in a new context. To illustrate how mirroring works, present the example of a child who is working on fine motor skill development. A teacher might directly work with a child on refining this skill through the use of table toys. To further help the child, the teacher might then provide a sieve and funnel for sand and water play. In addition, the teacher might ask the child to help pour juice for snack. All of these activities would be ways of mirroring the fine motor skill development.

Following this introduction, encourage the group to come up with their own examples of how mirroring takes place naturally in the classroom.

Activity: Selecting a Concept and Area for Mirroring

Introduce this activity with the direction that participants should now think about how they might use computers as a mirroring tool. Point out that computers can be especially effective mirrors because:

- Children can get as much reinforcement as they need and want at the computer.

- Children can work at their own pace.

- Software can present concepts in new ways and contexts.

- Practice with software can help children develop cognitive concepts to bridge the gulf between the real world and the abstract.

- Computer feedback can help reinforce learning.

- Most young children find working at the computer intrinsically motivating.

Begin by dividing participants into small groups of two or three. Assign each group the task of observing a classroom and then picking out a concept or skill that a child might be working on in one of the activity areas that could be mirrored through computers. Ideally, participants would observe children at play to see what tasks they are engaged in. If, however, the workshop is taking place at a time when no children are available for observation, encourage participants to walk around the classroom and reflect on how they've used the toys, props, and equipment to help children develop and/or refine skills and concepts.

Groups should target one particular skill or concept and then identify how a teacher would work with a child to promote development of that skill or concept in a given activity area. Then, by consulting and reviewing the provided software, participants should select software to mirror what the child was working on. For example, a teacher might work with a child in the table toy area on sequencing. With the teacher's guidance, the child could practice moving rectangular or triangular blocks around so that a chain of objects was made, ranging from biggest to smallest. To help the child learn how to make the bridge from the concrete world of table blocks to the more abstract world of symbols, the teacher could make use of any drawing programs using objects. The child, using this program, could then make triangles, rectangles, or circles of varying sizes, which could be moved into rows, ranging from largest to smallest. On the computer screen, the child is thus mirroring what was done in the table toy area.

As a culminating exercise, participants should write down some questions that they might ask a child while using the software. Handout #2 will guide participants through this task.

To conclude the workshop, ask participants to come up with an icon to represent the mirroring technique (e.g., a hand mirror) and add this group of software to the collection assembled in the previous workshop.

Handout #2: Mirror Planning

Concept or Skill Child Is Working On

Selected Activity Area and Activities for Developing Skill/Concept

Activity Planned for Computer Area (Including Chosen Software)

Questions to Promote Mirroring

XII. Outdoor Workshops

The outdoors is one of the most ignored settings for learning. Too often, outdoor time is viewed as the teacher's break time and an opportunity for children to run and let off steam. In a sense, it is a break for teachers—a time for them to be outdoors, have a change of scene, and interact with children in a different setting. It is also a place for children to run and stretch and use their "outside voices."

But the outdoor environment can offer much more for teachers and children. It doubles the learning environment and offers unique experiences. It is ideal for learning about nature, the changing seasons, and for gathering collections.

The purpose of providing workshops on the outdoors is to help teachers overcome any barriers they experience in using the outdoors and to give them a broader view of the many learning opportunities that can be provided.

Workshops: **Page**

The Importance of Outdoor Play 197

Creating the Outdoor Environment.. 202

The Teacher's Role 208

Handouts:

"Outdoor Safety Checklist" (Handout #1) 200

"Outdoor Observation" (Handout #2) 204

The Importance of Outdoor Play

Participants in this workshop will:

- explore their own attitudes toward the outdoor environment;

- identify the benefits of outdoor play for young children; and

- identify barriers and solutions to using the outdoor environment.

Materials needed:

- Chart pad, markers, and tape

Handout:

- "Outdoor Safety Checklist" (Handout #1)

Discussion: Attitudes about the Outdoors

Introduce the workshop by stating that the ways in which we use the outdoor environment with young children are greatly influenced by how we ourselves feel about the outdoors.

Lead participants in a discussion about how they feel about the outdoors by asking the following questions:

- "What do you remember enjoying most about playing outdoors when you were a child? What did you enjoy least?"

- "As an adult, what do you enjoy most about being outdoors?"

Here's what you might hear:

- "I liked playing in dirt (or mud, water, or sand) when I was a child."

- "I liked riding my bike with a friend."

- "I always felt safer indoors."

- "There was a quiet place I could go to and be alone and think."

- "I like being outdoors doing something, like working in the garden."

- "Sometimes I just like to sit outside and read a book."

Emphasize that it can be helpful to examine how we feel about the outdoors for two reasons. First, children are sensitive to adult feelings and can be influenced by what we feel about the outdoors. Second, the things that we enjoy about the outdoors are often the same things that children enjoy.

Activity: Exploring the Learning Opportunities Outdoors

The following activity will give participants a chance to identify some of the many learning opportunities available outdoors. Ask participants to select a partner for a 20-minute walk through the playground or surrounding neighborhood. Ask each team to look for ways that the outdoors can be used to promote:

- an understanding of science and nature;
- the development of classification skills; and
- aesthetic appreciation.

When the group returns, list their discoveries on the chart pad. Here are some examples of what participants may identify on their walk.

- For science and nature:

    rain water evaporating,
    buds appearing on the trees,
    worms under a rock, and
    clouds moving in the sky.

- For classification skills:

    seed collections,
    rock collections to sort, and
    leaves of different sizes and shapes.

- For aesthetic appreciation:

    the colors of the flowers,
    reflections of the sun, and
    how the wind blows the leaves on the trees.

Next, ask participants to think about how their observations would differ in another environment. What different opportunities would another setting provide?

Summarize the exercise by making the following points:

- Outdoors, children have unique opportunities to observe nature firsthand, to explore, and to enjoy the freedom of space and movement.

- The outdoors is an evolving learning environment. It may contain many raw materials such as grass, dirt, and water that are naturally appealing to young children.

Activity: Barriers and Solutions to Using the Outdoor Environment

Teachers face typical problems that may prevent them from using the outdoors effectively. Finding realistic solutions to these barriers can help teachers enjoy the outdoors more and convey their enthusiasm to children.

Brainstorm as a group about all the problems or barriers that get in the way of making the outdoors a rich environment for learning. Then form groups of four and ask each group to identify solutions to the problems. Reconvene the entire group to hear reports on solutions identified. As each group reports, note the ideas on a chart pad. Here's an example of what you might record.

BARRIERS	SOLUTIONS
Too cold	Wear appropriate clothing Keep active outdoors Keep extra mittens and hats for children and adults
Not enough time	Schedule outdoor time as part of the daily routine Allow sufficient time for children to put on coats and other accessories and to take them off
Not enough teachers to supervise	Recognize that teachers need a break but not during outdoor time Coordinate outdoor schedules with other classes to maximize supervision
Not enough to do outdoors	Bring some indoor activities outside each day Learn group games you can play Identify places nearby that offer variety

Summarize the discussion by emphasizing the importance of planning for outdoor time to overcome barriers so that the outdoors can become a rich learning environment.

Assignment:

In preparation for the next session, ask participants to draw a map of their outdoor play area. Have them include a list of all equipment and materials available.

Next, distribute and review the "Outdoor Safety Checklist" (Handout #1). Ask participants to use the form to evaluate the safety of their own outdoor area or of any public playground that they use. Ask them to also share the checklist with their program director, develop a plan to remedy any problems they discover, and bring the completed form to the next session.

Handout #1: Outdoor Safety Checklist

                                                                          Yes   No

Physical Layout

- Is the space large enough to accommodate all the children in the group? Most experts recommend 80 to 100 square feet per child.

- Is the space between pieces of equipment large enough so that children aren't running into each other?

- Is the slide in a shaded area where it won't get too hot?

- Is the ground cover soft under swings, climbing toys, and slides?

- Have drainage areas, electrical wires, and other hazardous equipment been covered?

- Is the area free of debris and obstacles?

- Are all riding paths clearly marked, gently curved, and separate from large group areas?

Equipment

- Is all the equipment solid and in good repair? (There should be no rusted bolts or protruding nails, peeling paint, loose screws, or splintered wood.)

- Does the equipment have appropriate material under it (i.e., sand or grass that is absorbent and able to cushion falls)?

- Does the slide curve at the bottom to become parallel to the ground?

- Are the slide handles in good repair and at the correct level for preschoolers?

- Are the slide platforms at least five feet high, and do they have protective railings around them?

- Is all equipment scaled to size for young children?

- Is all equipment free of sharp points, corners, and edges?

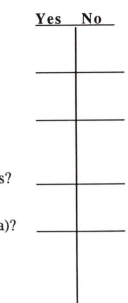

Yes   No

- Are all tricycles and wheel toys in good repair (screws tightened, handlebars secure)?

- Is the sandbox clean and free of broken toys? Is the sandbox covered when not in use?

Supervision

- Do teachers have unobstructed views of children at all times?

- Is an adult assigned to each active area of the play space (e.g., climbing equipment, riding areas, woodworking area)?

- Do adults supervise the children at all times?

- Are there established rules that children understand and follow (e.g., not to run in front of the swings)?

Note Any Improvements Needed

_____

_____

_____

_____

_____

_____

_____

Creating the Outdoor Environment

Participants in this workshop will:

- share the results of their assessment of the safety of their outdoor environments;

- identify outdoor activity areas; and

- explore new ways to use their outdoor space creatively.

Materials needed:

- Chart pad, markers, and tape

- *The Creative Curriculum* videotape and VCR

- Participants' completed "Outdoor Safety Checklist" and sketches of their outdoor areas

Handout:

- "Outdoor Observation" form (Handout #2)

Discussion: Sharing of Safety Checklists

Allow time at the beginning of the workshop for participants to share the results of their safety checks. You might pose the following questions:

- "How did your outdoor environment measure up on safety?"

- "Were there any surprises?"

- "What changes, if any, do you feel need to be made?"

Safety is, of course, the primary consideration. After ensuring that it is a safe place for children, we can look at the outdoor environment as an integral part of the total learning environment. The outdoor time should be planned as carefully as the indoor time.

Activity: Identifying Outdoor Activity Areas

List on chart paper the seven outdoor activity areas included in the *Creative Curriculum*:

- climbing,
- digging and pouring,
- riding,
- an area for quiet play,
- an area for pets,
- gardening, and
- woodworking.

Have participants identify any other areas that they have in their outdoor environments and add them to the list.

To illustrate how these activity areas really work, show the outdoors portion of the *Creative Curriculum* videotape. Note that many of the activity areas shown were either created by teachers or expanded with the addition of homemade materials. Participants will see the following examples on the tape:

- blowing bubbles outdoors;
- painting a building with water; and
- bringing cardboard boxes outside.

After viewing the videotape, ask participants to take out the drawings of their outdoor environments and identify where the different activities take place.

- "Where do children climb?"
- "Where can children dig?"
- "Where could a child play quietly alone?"

Point out which areas seem to be forgotten. You may find, for example, that woodworking is missing or that no specific space is designated for quiet play. Ask participants to identify the areas most frequently used by the children and why they think this is so.

Next, have participants select a partner and choose an area that they would like to develop or expand for their own outdoor area. Ask them to develop a plan for how they will do this, including the following information:

- where to locate the area;

- what would have to be purchased to equip the area; and

- what teachers and parents could donate or make to help equip the area.

Refer participants to the module in the *Creative Curriculum* on Outdoors for additional ideas on setting up individual activity areas.

Allow approximately 15 to 20 minutes and then ask each team to share its plans with the whole group. Summarize the discussion by pointing out the main advantages of organizing the outdoors into distinct activity areas:

- Children can choose from a variety of activities.

- The areas provide a balance between active and quiet play; group and individual play; teacher-directed and child-initiated play.

- Although some equipment within an activity area may stay the same (i.e., the climbing apparatus or the sand box), what children do within the area is constantly evolving as the props and seasons change and as children grow and develop new skills and interests.

Assignment:

Distribute the "Outdoor Observation" form (Handout #2) and review it with participants. Ask them to complete the form and bring it to the next session.

Handout #2: Outdoor Observation

Introduction:

To use the outdoors most effectively, the best place to begin is by observing children's use of the outdoor environment. Start by observing one child. By following a child for 10 to 15 minutes periodically, you can collect data on what the child is doing, the materials the child uses, who the child likes to play with, and the developmental capabilities of that child in each of the outdoor interest areas.

Select one child to observe over a one-week period and note where the child plays outdoors and what he or she does.

Name of Child: _____

Age: _____ **Week of Observation**: _____

General Observations

What play areas does the child use?

What specific equipment does the child use?

Are there play areas that the child avoids?

Is there specific equipment that the child avoids?

Does the child interact with others? Who initiates play?

How are conflicts resolved?

How long does the child play in each area?

Does the child use the equipment/area in creative ways? (Give examples.)

Does the child ask for help? Whom does the child ask (adults or children)?

Does the child act differently (e.g., in terms of language, social skills, physical skills) outdoors than indoors?

What is the child specifically interested in (e.g., trees, sand, seasons, wind)?

Observing in the large muscle areas

Does the child use the equipment? Which pieces? How well?

Does the child try new things with the equipment or continually practice old skills?

Does the child engage in dramatic play on the equipment? What roles does he or she play?

Does the child ask for help?

Observing in the digging and pouring area

What props (pails, bowls, cars) does the child use?

How long does the child stay in the sand area? Does the child need to be encouraged to try something new?

Does the child explore different possibilities for solving problems?

Observing in the riding area

Can the child use the riding toys? Which ones?

How well does the child use the riding toys (i.e., how capable is the child of controlling speed, turning corners, or riding through obstacle courses)?

Can the child take turns with the equipment?

Observing in the quiet area

What activities in the quiet area does the child enjoy the most—games, art, imagery, books, songs?

Does the child rest and "cool off" if needed?

Observing in the gardening and pet areas

Is the child careful and loving with animals?

Does the child take an interest in the garden?

Observing in the woodworking area

What tools is the child able to use? How well?

Does the child share and work with others?

Is the child aware of safety rules and able to follow them?

The Teacher's Role

Participants in this workshop will:

• identify how outdoor play contributes to social, physical, emotional, and cognitive development; and

• identify ways that teachers can help children use the outdoors in imaginative and creative ways.

Materials needed:

• Chart pad, markers, and tape

• Participants' completed "Outdoor Observation" forms

Discussion: How Outdoor Play Contributes to Growth and Development

Begin the session by inviting participants to share the observations of a child. What did they learn? Ask for examples from their own observations of how outdoor play contributes to social, physical, emotional, and cognitive development. Record the ideas on a chart pad. (Refer participants to the goals and objectives outlined in the module on Outdoors if necessary.)

Social Development	Emotional Development	Physical Development	Cognitive Development

Listed below are examples of what you may hear.

Social Development

• Take turns, negotiate, and compromise.

• Cooperate in group games.

• Engage in dramatic play.

Emotional Development

- Develop a sense of pride in their accomplishments.

- Gain independence as they learn to use equipment.

Physical Development

- Explore and discover what their bodies can do.

- Develop and refine large muscle skills.

- Improve their health by being in the fresh air every day.

Cognitive Development

- Develop language skills.

- Observe many cause-and-effect relationships in nature.

- Solve problems, plan, and experiment with new ideas.

Activity: Using the Outdoors Creatively

Emphasize that an important part of the teacher's role outdoors is to help children use the environment in creative and imaginative ways. Divide participants into four groups and assign each group one of the following tasks:

- How could you create a dramatic play theme outdoors? What materials would you provide? How would you get children involved?

- Design two water play experiences that could only take place outdoors. What props would you need? How would you set up these experiences?

- How many different things do you think children could do with hoops, balls, and rope?

- If you had nothing but an open, grassy area for outdoor play, what could you bring outdoors to create an interesting environment?

Allow 20 minutes for this activity and then have each group report. Emphasize the following points:

- The teacher helps create the outdoor environment by providing children with the props they need for play.

- Any outdoor space that you have available can be used creatively when you plan for the environment.

- The outdoor environment naturally changes throughout the year. This provides even more opportunities to create an exciting learning environment.

End the session by referring participants to the *Creative Curriculum* for additional ideas. Encourage them to visit other nearby preschool and kindergarten programs to see different outdoor areas and get new ideas for their own space.

Appendices

A. *Creative Curriculum* **Self-Assessment and Observation Form**

B. **Staff Development Forms**

Appendix A

Creative Curriculum
Self-Assessment and Observation Form

Creative Curriculum
Self-Assessment and Observation Form

The *Creative Curriculum* Self-Assessment and Observation Form can serve as the focus for planning ongoing staff development. The process requires a full commitment from both the teacher and supervisor to support individual growth.

To the teacher:

This task takes about an hour and helps you to consider the full range of job expectations involved in effectively implementing *The Creative Curriculum for Early Childhood*. In this self-assessment process, you will rank how much you value each statement and how well you feel you demonstrate each one.

The "Job Expectations" are statements of knowledge and skills required to effectively implement the *Creative Curriculum*. You can complete the self-assessment in three stages.

First, look over each statement briefly to see what it says. Do not ponder each one.

Second, review each statement again and ask yourself which you consider **most** valuable for carrying out your job, which are **somewhat** valuable, and which are **least** valuable. You may value all of the job expectations noted. However, this process is most effective if you honestly consider which are most important to you and which you see as less valuable. Record your assessment for each statement by placing a mark on the lines where you think you belong.

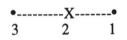

Third, repeat the process, this time assessing to what degree you feel you possess and demonstrate each of the job expectations. Again, be honest with yourself. Completing the self-assessment is the first step in designing staff development tailored to meet your individual needs and interests.

To the supervisor:

After the teacher has completed the self-assessment, arrange a convenient time to observe in the classroom. You can do an overall observation on all the items listed, or focus your observations on a particular cluster of expectations. This is something you can decide with the teacher. Record your observations by placing a mark on the line where you think the teacher belongs. Record any additional comments in the space provided below the line.

Shortly after the observation, plan a time to meet with the teacher to review each of your ratings. Decide on priorities for staff development. These decisions will be influenced by what the teacher values most but feels least skilled in performing, as well as your assessment of what is in the best interest of the children.

Once you have agreed on the focus for staff development, discuss the variety of options for offering support and develop a plan outlining what each of you will do and by when. Forms for staff development are included in Appendix B.

Creative Curriculum Self-Assessment and Observation Form

Teacher: _____

Date of Self-Assessment: _____

Supervisor: _____

Date(s) of Observation: _____

Teacher's Self Assessment	Job Expectations	Supervisor's Observations and Comments
ORGANIZING THE ENVIRONMENT		
Value 3 — 2 — 1 Demonstrate 3 — 2 — 1	Organize the environment into clearly defined areas and display props, accessories, and materials where they are to be used.	3 — 2 — 1
Value 3 — 2 — 1 Demonstrate 3 — 2 — 1	Arrange the areas so that children can play on their own and in small groups.	3 — 2 — 1
Value 3 — 2 — 1 Demonstrate 3 — 2 — 1	Select and use equipment and materials that are safe, scaled to size, well-maintained, and developmentally appropriate.	3 — 2 — 1
Value 3 — 2 — 1 Demonstrate 3 — 2 — 1	Separate noisy areas from quiet ones.	3 — 2 — 1
Value 3 — 2 — 1 Demonstrate 3 — 2 — 1	Make adjustments as needed for children with disabilities.	3 — 2 — 1
Value 3 — 2 — 1 Demonstrate 3 — 2 — 1	Expand and enrich children's play by adding new materials, equipment, and props to each interest area regularly.	3 — 2 — 1
Value 3 — 2 — 1 Demonstrate 3 — 2 — 1	Display materials simply and attractively with picture labels on shelves and on storage containers.	3 — 2 — 1

Key:

Value	Demonstrate	Observation by Supervisor
3 = highest	3 = always	3 = always
1 = lowest	2 = sometimes	2 = sometimes
	1 = rarely	1 = rarely

Creative Curriculum Self-Assessment and Observation Form

Teacher: _____

Date of Self-Assessment: _____

Supervisor: _____

Date(s) of Observation: _____

Teacher's Self Assessment	Job Expectations	Supervisor's Observations and Comments
ORGANIZING THE ENVIRONMENT (Cont'd)		
Value 3 — 2 — 1 Demonstrate 3 — 2 — 1	Provide soft spaces such as pillows, rugs, bean bags, and soft materials such as dough, sand, and water.	3 — 2 — 1
PLANNING AN APPROPRIATE DAILY PROGRAM		
Value 3 — 2 — 1 Demonstrate 3 — 2 — 1	Include in the daily schedule active and quiet times, group and individual activities, teacher-led and child-initiated activities, and indoor and outdoor play.	3 — 2 — 1
Value 3 — 2 — 1 Demonstrate 3 — 2 — 1	Plan time periods appropriate to the ages and experiences of the children (e.g., 5-10 minute group times for young 3's and longer group times for 4- and 5-year-olds).	3 — 2 — 1
Value 3 — 2 — 1 Demonstrate 3 — 2 — 1	Maintain a consistent schedule that does not sacrifice flexibility when needed, and routines that enable children to predict events and develop a basic sense of trust.	3 — 2 — 1
Value 3 — 2 — 1 Demonstrate 3 — 2 — 1	Use available community resources such as special guests or field trips, to expand and extend children's experiences.	3 — 2 — 1
Value 3 — 2 — 1 Demonstrate 3 — 2 — 1	Allow at least an hour or more for self-selected activities that allow children to initiate play in all learning areas as they interact with materials, other children, and adults.	3 — 2 — 1

Key:

Value
3 = highest
1 = lowest

Demonstrate
3 = always
2 = sometimes
1 = rarely

Observation by Supervisor
3 = always
2 = sometimes
1 = rarely

Creative Curriculum Self-Assessment and Observation Form

Teacher: _____

Date of Self-Assessment: _____

Supervisor: _____

Date(s) of Observation: _____

Teacher's Self Assessment	Job Expectations	Supervisor's Observations and Comments
PLANNING AN APPROPRIATE DAILY PROGRAM (Cont'd)		
Value 3 — 2 — 1 Demonstrate 3 — 2 — 1	Implement family-style mealtimes and help children socialize, serve themselves, and assist in setting and cleaning the tables.	3 — 2 — 1
USING TRANSITION TIMES FOR LEARNING		
Value 3 — 2 — 1 Demonstrate 3 — 2 — 1	Give children a sufficient warning before announcing clean-up time.	3 — 2 — 1
Value 3 — 2 — 1 Demonstrate 3 — 2 — 1	When needed, allow children additional time to complete activities before moving on to the next scheduled activity.	3 — 2 — 1
Value 3 — 2 — 1 Demonstrate 3 — 2 — 1	Use songs, finger plays, and stories to ease transition times.	3 — 2 — 1
Value 3 — 2 — 1 Demonstrate 3 — 2 — 1	Involve children in setting up activities and cleaning up.	3 — 2 — 1
Value 3 — 2 — 1 Demonstrate 3 — 2 — 1	Use clean up as a time for helping children learn to discriminate, match, and classify objects.	3 — 2 — 1

Key:

Value
3 = highest
1 = lowest

Demonstrate
3 = always
2 = sometimes
1 = rarely

Observation by Supervisor
3 = always
2 = sometimes
1 = rarely

Creative Curriculum Self-Assessment and Observation Form

Teacher: _____

Date of Self-Assessment: _____

Supervisor: _____

Date(s) of Observation: _____

Teacher's Self Assessment	Job Expectations	Supervisor's Observations and Comments
SUPPORTING CHILDREN'S SOCIO-EMOTIONAL DEVELOPMENT		
Value 3 — 2 — 1 Demonstrate 3 — 2 — 1	Spend individual time with each child each day.	3 — 2 — 1
Value 3 — 2 — 1 Demonstrate 3 — 2 — 1	Help children develop responsibility and independence by labeling shelves, using a picture schedule and job chart, and making materials accessible to them.	3 — 2 — 1
Value 3 — 2 — 1 Demonstrate 3 — 2 — 1	Include pictures and materials that reflect diversity (ethnic, gender, ability, age).	3 — 2 — 1
Value 3 — 2 — 1 Demonstrate 3 — 2 — 1	Talk with children in ways that show respect and caring and build optimum self-esteem.	3 — 2 — 1
Value 3 — 2 — 1 Demonstrate 3 — 2 — 1	Offer encouragement, guidance, and reinforcement for efforts and accomplishments.	3 — 2 — 1
Value 3 — 2 — 1 Demonstrate 3 — 2 — 1	Establish consistent rules and behavioral expectations and convey them clearly and consistently	3 — 2 — 1

Key:

Value
3 = highest
1 = lowest

Demonstrate
3 = always
2 = sometimes
1 = rarely

Observation by Supervisor
3 = always
2 = sometimes
1 = rarely

Creative Curriculum **Self-Assessment and Observation Form**

Teacher: _____

Date of Self-Assessment: _____

Supervisor: _____

Date(s) of Observation: _____

Teacher's Self Assessment	Job Expectations	Supervisor's Observations and Comments
SUPPORTING CHILDREN'S SOCIO-EMOTIONAL DEVELOPMENT (Cont'd)		
Value 3 — 2 — 1 Demonstrate 3 — 2 — 1	Help children resolve conflicts by using a problem-solving approach.	3 — 2 — 1
Value 3 — 2 — 1 Demonstrate 3 — 2 — 1	Prepare a protected place for each child's belongings, such as a cubby with the child's picture and name.	3 — 2 — 1
Value 3 — 2 — 1 Demonstrate 3 — 2 — 1	Provide a way to display and protect each child's completed work.	3 — 2 — 1
EXTENDING CHILDREN'S THINKING		
Value 3 — 2 — 1 Demonstrate 3 — 2 — 1	Actively participate in and reinforce children's play.	3 — 2 — 1
Value 3 — 2 — 1 Demonstrate 3 — 2 — 1	Talk with children about their work focusing on the process, providing new vocabulary, and reinforcing their efforts.	3 — 2 — 1
Value 3 — 2 — 1 Demonstrate 3 — 2 — 1	Promote problem solving by asking children open-ended questions and making suggestions.	3 — 2 — 1

Key:

Value
3 = highest
1 = lowest

Demonstrate
3 = always
2 = sometimes
1 = rarely

Observation by Supervisor
3 = always
2 = sometimes
1 = rarely

Creative Curriculum Self-Assessment and Observation Form

Teacher: _____   Supervisor: _____

Date of Self-Assessment: _____   Date(s) of Observation: _____

Teacher's Self Assessment	Job Expectations	Supervisor's Observations and Comments
EXTENDING CHILDREN'S THINKING (Cont'd)		
Value ●·····●·····● 3 2 1 Demonstrate ●·····●·····● 3 2 1	Plan challenging and appropriate activities in response to children's changing needs, interests and skills.	●·····●·····● 3 2 1
PROMOTING CHILDREN'S PHYSICAL DEVELOPMENT		
Value ●·····●·····● 3 2 1 Demonstrate ●·····●·····● 3 2 1	Plan activities that help children develop small muscle control (e.g., drawing, cutting, stringing beads).	●·····●·····● 3 2 1
Value ●·····●·····● 3 2 1 Demonstrate ●·····●·····● 3 2 1	Plan activities that promote large muscle development (e.g., jump rope, climbing, dancing, playing with balls).	●·····●·····● 3 2 1
Value ●·····●·····● 3 2 1 Demonstrate ●·····●·····● 3 2 1	Provide opportunities for children to use all their senses to explore and understand their world.	●·····●·····● 3 2 1
Value ●·····●·····● 3 2 1 Demonstrate ●·····●·····● 3 2 1	Establish an environment in which children want to engage in physical activities.	●·····●·····● 3 2 1
Value ●·····●·····● 3 2 1 Demonstrate ●·····●·····● 3 2 1	Plan outdoor activities that allow children to use large and small muscles during individual play and group experiences.	●·····●·····● 3 2 1

Key:

Value
3 = highest
1 = lowest

Demonstrate
3 = always
2 = sometimes
1 = rarely

Observation by Supervisor
3 = always
2 = sometimes
1 = rarely

Creative Curriculum Self-Assessment and Observation Form

Teacher: _____

Date of Self-Assessment: _____

Supervisor: _____

Date(s) of Observation: _____

Teacher's Self Assessment	Job Expectations	Supervisor's Observations and Comments
PROMOTING CHILDREN'S PHYSICAL DEVELOPMENT (Cont'd)		
Value 3 — 2 — 1 Demonstrate 3 — 2 — 1	Acknowledge children's accomplishments as they attempt to learn new skills.	3 — 2 — 1
INDIVIDUALIZING THE PROGRAM		
Value 3 — 2 — 1 Demonstrate 3 — 2 — 1	Demonstrate knowledge of the stages of children's development in all areas.	3 — 2 — 1
Value 3 — 2 — 1 Demonstrate 3 — 2 — 1	Use the *Creative Curriculum* Child Development and Learning Checklist and collections of children's work to assess each child's development.	3 — 2 — 1
Value 3 — 2 — 1 Demonstrate 3 — 2 — 1	Use assessment information to plan activities that promote each child's growth and development.	3 — 2 — 1
Value 3 — 2 — 1 Demonstrate 3 — 2 — 1	Recognize and allow for individual differences in development and abilities when planning activities/learning experiences.	3 — 2 — 1
Value 3 — 2 — 1 Demonstrate 3 — 2 — 1	Use on-going observation of children in activity areas to modify and enrich the learning environment.	3 — 2 — 1

Key:

Value	Demonstrate	Observation by Supervisor
3 = highest	3 = always	3 = always
1 = lowest	2 = sometimes	2 = sometimes
	1 = rarely	1 = rarely

Creative Curriculum Self-Assessment and Observation Form

Teacher: _____

Date of Self-Assessment: _____

Supervisor: _____

Date(s) of Observation: _____

Teacher's Self Assessment	Job Expectations	Supervisor's Observations and Comments
INDIVIDUALIZING THE PROGRAM (Cont'd)		
Value 3 2 1 Demonstrate 3 2 1	Integrate concepts and themes that reflect the community and the interests of the children.	3 2 1
Value 3 2 1 Demonstrate 3 2 1	Prepare weekly and long-term plans, collect materials, and prepare the environment to reflect the needs and interests of children in the group.	3 2 1
THE BLOCK CORNER		
Value 3 2 1 Demonstrate 3 2 1	Provide a complete set of unit blocks, including the four unit sizes; a variety of pillars, triangles, cylinders, ramps, and curves; arches, buttresses, and switches; and roof boards.	3 2 1
Value 3 2 1 Demonstrate 3 2 1	Organize the blocks lengthwise and by shape and size on labeled shelves.	3 2 1
Value 3 2 1 Demonstrate 3 2 1	Extend block building by adding new blocks and accessories, providing books and other materials to promote new themes.	3 2 1
Value 3 2 1 Demonstrate 3 2 1	Support and extend children's efforts to recreate experiences (such as a recent field trip) and try out various roles (such as a bus driver, firefighter, or zoo attendant).	3 2 1

Key:

Value
3 = highest
1 = lowest

Demonstrate
3 = always
2 = sometimes
1 = rarely

Observation by Supervisor
3 = always
2 = sometimes
1 = rarely

Creative Curriculum Self-Assessment and Observation Form

Teacher: _____

Date of Self-Assessment: _____

Supervisor: _____

Date(s) of Observation: _____

Teacher's Self Assessment	Job Expectations	Supervisor's Observations and Comments
THE BLOCK CORNER (Cont'd)		
Value 3 — 2 — 1 Demonstrate 3 — 2 — 1	Promote problem solving with blocks by asking questions to extend children's thinking and ideas.	3 — 2 — 1
Value 3 — 2 — 1 Demonstrate 3 — 2 — 1	Point out the mathematical relationships and geometric shapes of the blocks.	3 — 2 — 1
THE HOUSE CORNER		
Value 3 — 2 — 1 Demonstrate 3 — 2 — 1	Set up a homelike and inviting house corner by using furniture to create an enclosed space and by adding props that reflect the children's experiences and backgrounds.	3 — 2 — 1
Value 3 — 2 — 1 Demonstrate 3 — 2 — 1	Provide accessories to promote role playing by children, such as cooking, eating, and cleaning utensils, clothes and hats, and pocketbooks, suitcases, and keys.	3 — 2 — 1
Value 3 — 2 — 1 Demonstrate 3 — 2 — 1	Expand the house corner to enrich children's play by adding new props and furniture (e.g., for a supermarket, laundromat, shoe store, or doctor's office).	3 — 2 — 1
Value 3 — 2 — 1 Demonstrate 3 — 2 — 1	Teach children how to play: to make-believe with objects and events, to stay involved with a play theme.	3 — 2 — 1

Key:

Value
3 = highest
1 = lowest

Demonstrate
3 = always
2 = sometimes
1 = rarely

Observation by Supervisor
3 = always
2 = sometimes
1 = rarely

Appendix A

225

Creative Curriculum Self-Assessment and Observation Form

Teacher: _____

Date of Self-Assessment: _____

Supervisor: _____

Date(s) of Observation: _____

Teacher's Self Assessment	Job Expectations	Supervisor's Observations and Comments
THE HOUSE CORNER (Cont'd)		
Value 3 — 2 — 1 Demonstrate 3 — 2 — 1	Help children to work together in cooperative play by suggesting roles and participating in their play as needed.	3 — 2 — 1
THE TABLE TOY AREA		
Value 3 — 2 — 1 Demonstrate 3 — 2 — 1	Provide a balance of self-correcting and open-ended table toys.	3 — 2 — 1
Value 3 — 2 — 1 Demonstrate 3 — 2 — 1	Provide table toys with a variety of attributes such as color, shape, size, number, order, and position.	3 — 2 — 1
Value 3 — 2 — 1 Demonstrate 3 — 2 — 1	Suggest alternative ways to use toys such as providing children with pattern cards, matrix boards, and categorizing circles, and by organizing simple games.	3 — 2 — 1
Value 3 — 2 — 1 Demonstrate 3 — 2 — 1	Add to supply of table toys with collected materials such as buttons, keys, bottle tops, thread spools, plastic bread closures, and homemade matching games.	3 — 2 — 1
Value 3 — 2 — 1 Demonstrate 3 — 2 — 1	Introduce table toys to children and ask questions to encourage them to think of new ways to use toys.	3 — 2 — 1

Key:

Value
3 = highest
1 = lowest

Demonstrate
3 = always
2 = sometimes
1 = rarely

Observation by Supervisor
3 = always
2 = sometimes
1 = rarely

Creative Curriculum Self-Assessment and Observation Form

Teacher: _____

Supervisor: _____

Date of Self-Assessment: _____

Date(s) of Observation: _____

Teacher's Self Assessment	Job Expectations	Supervisor's Observations and Comments
THE ART AREA		
Value 3 — 2 — 1 Demonstrate 3 — 2 — 1	Include materials in the art area for writing and drawing, painting, pasting, printing, and molding.	3 — 2 — 1
Value 3 — 2 — 1 Demonstrate 3 — 2 — 1	Avoid the use of precut shapes and coloring books as art activities.	3 — 2 — 1
Value 3 — 2 — 1 Demonstrate 3 — 2 — 1	Provide new materials to stimulate creativity and experimentation.	3 — 2 — 1
Value 3 — 2 — 1 Demonstrate 3 — 2 — 1	Plan occasional craft activities such as weaving, stitchery, and puppet making according to children's skill levels and interests.	3 — 2 — 1
Value 3 — 2 — 1 Demonstrate 3 — 2 — 1	Encourage on-going exploration of a variety of art materials.	3 — 2 — 1
Value 3 — 2 — 1 Demonstrate 3 — 2 — 1	Allow children to express their own ideas freely through art.	3 — 2 — 1

Key:

Value
3 = highest
1 = lowest

Demonstrate
3 = always
2 = sometimes
1 = rarely

Observation by Supervisor
3 = always
2 = sometimes
1 = rarely

Creative Curriculum Self-Assessment and Observation Form

Teacher: _____

Supervisor: _____

Date of Self-Assessment: _____

Date(s) of Observation: _____

Teacher's Self Assessment	Job Expectations	Supervisor's Observations and Comments
THE LIBRARY CORNER		
Value 3 — 2 — 1 Demonstrate 3 — 2 — 1	Select books that reflect the children's life experiences, concerns, and interests.	3 — 2 — 1
Value 3 — 2 — 1 Demonstrate 3 — 2 — 1	Read books to children every day.	3 — 2 — 1
Value 3 — 2 — 1 Demonstrate 3 — 2 — 1	Display books attractively so children can see the covers.	3 — 2 — 1
Value 3 — 2 — 1 Demonstrate 3 — 2 — 1	Rotate books adding new ones each week.	3 — 2 — 1
Value 3 — 2 — 1 Demonstrate 3 — 2 — 1	Visit the library area at least once during every free play period, validating the importance of the area.	3 — 2 — 1
Value 3 — 2 — 1 Demonstrate 3 — 2 — 1	Make cassette tapes of stories and include story tapes in the listening area.	3 — 2 — 1

Key:

Value
3 = highest
1 = lowest

Demonstrate
3 = always
2 = sometimes
1 = rarely

Observation by Supervisor
3 = always
2 = sometimes
1 = rarely

Appendix A

Creative Curriculum Self-Assessment and Observation Form

Teacher: _____
Date of Self-Assessment: _____

Supervisor: _____
Date(s) of Observation: _____

Teacher's Self Assessment	Job Expectations	Supervisor's Observations and Comments
THE LIBRARY CORNER (Cont'd)		
Value: 3 — 2 — 1 Demonstrate: 3 — 2 — 1	Use the book and listening areas to spend time with just one child or a few children.	3 — 2 — 1
SAND AND WATER		
Value: 3 — 2 — 1 Demonstrate: 3 — 2 — 1	Maintain sand and water—check temperature, consistency, and cleanliness.	3 — 2 — 1
Value: 3 — 2 — 1 Demonstrate: 3 — 2 — 1	Add props to encourage children to measure, compare, experiment, and discover.	3 — 2 — 1
Value: 3 — 2 — 1 Demonstrate: 3 — 2 — 1	Check the condition of props periodically and replace them as needed.	3 — 2 — 1
Value: 3 — 2 — 1 Demonstrate: 3 — 2 — 1	Talk with children about what they are discovering and encourage their play.	3 — 2 — 1
Value: 3 — 2 — 1 Demonstrate: 3 — 2 — 1	Provide equipment and materials for cleaning up the sand and water area (e.g., sponges, mops, brooms).	3 — 2 — 1

Key:

Value
- 3 = highest
- 1 = lowest

Demonstrate
- 3 = always
- 2 = sometimes
- 1 = rarely

Observation by Supervisor
- 3 = always
- 2 = sometimes
- 1 = rarely

Creative Curriculum Self-Assessment and Observation Form

Teacher: _____

Date of Self-Assessment: _____

Supervisor: _____

Date(s) of Observation: _____

Teacher's Self Assessment	Job Expectations	Supervisor's Observations and Comments
MUSIC AND MOVEMENT		
Value 3 2 1 Demonstrate 3 2 1	Allocate space for movement and music activities and provide musical instruments, a tape recorder, and a variety of props.	3 2 1
Value 3 2 1 Demonstrate 3 2 1	Use the outdoors as well as the indoor area for movement and dance activities.	3 2 1
Value 3 2 1 Demonstrate 3 2 1	Provide materials for children to listen to music and songs, including easy-to-operate tape recorders and earphones, shelf space for tapes, and picture/word labels to identify tapes.	3 2 1
Value 3 2 1 Demonstrate 3 2 1	Select a variety of tapes (e.g., music that is fast and lively, slow and soothing; children's songs and folk music, music from the cultures represented by children in the group as well as from other cultures, lullabies, classical music, jazz, rock, opera, and current "hits").	3 2 1
Value 3 2 1 Demonstrate 3 2 1	Provide musical instruments for children to try out various sounds and to stage parades, circuses, and shows, including drums, rhythm sticks, cymbals, kazoos, tambourines, triangles, maracas, shakers, rattles, sand blocks, and bells.	3 2 1
Value 3 2 1 Demonstrate 3 2 1	Sing songs and use recorded music to "set a tone" for the room, to help children change their activity levels, and to help them move from one activity to another (e.g., free play to clean up, clean up to circle time).	3 2 1

Key:

Value
3 = highest
1 = lowest

Demonstrate
3 = always
2 = sometimes
1 = rarely

Observation by Supervisor
3 = always
2 = sometimes
1 = rarely

Creative Curriculum Self-Assessment and Observation Form

Teacher: _____

Supervisor: _____

Date of Self-Assessment: _____

Date(s) of Observation: _____

Teacher's Self Assessment	Job Expectations	Supervisor's Observations and Comments
COOKING		
Value: 3 — 2 — 1 Demonstrate: 3 — 2 — 1	Create portable cooking boxes for readily incorporating cooking into the program, if a stand-alone cooking area cannot be created.	3 — 2 — 1
Value: 3 — 2 — 1 Demonstrate: 3 — 2 — 1	Set up the environment with real cooking appliances, gadgets, and utensils.	3 — 2 — 1
Value: 3 — 2 — 1 Demonstrate: 3 — 2 — 1	Develop picture-based recipe cards to promote independent use of cooking activities.	3 — 2 — 1
Value: 3 — 2 — 1 Demonstrate: 3 — 2 — 1	Provide adequate supervision of cooking activities that might be potentially dangerous, such as cooking with heat or using a grinder or blender.	3 — 2 — 1
Value: 3 — 2 — 1 Demonstrate: 3 — 2 — 1	Promote respect for cultural diversity by including cooking activities that reflect the children's backgrounds/asking parents for recipe ideas/encouraging parents to lead classroom cooking activities.	3 — 2 — 1

Key:

Value
3 = highest
1 = lowest

Demonstrate
3 = always
2 = sometimes
1 = rarely

Observation by Supervisor
3 = always
2 = sometimes
1 = rarely

Creative Curriculum Self-Assessment and Observation Form

Teacher: _____

Date of Self-Assessment: _____

Supervisor: _____

Date(s) of Observation: _____

Teacher's Self Assessment	Job Expectations	Supervisor's Observations and Comments
COMPUTERS		
Value 3 – 2 – 1 Demonstrate 3 – 2 – 1	Set up the computer area in a place that is out of the line of traffic, where children can discuss things quietly and concentrate on what they are doing.	3 – 2 – 1
Value 3 – 2 – 1 Demonstrate 3 – 2 – 1	Introduce children to the computer individually or in pairs so that children can learn to operate the equipment on their own.	3 – 2 – 1
Value 3 – 2 – 1 Demonstrate 3 – 2 – 1	Encourage children to use the computer in pairs, to promote social development.	3 – 2 – 1
Value 3 – 2 – 1 Demonstrate 3 – 2 – 1	Know how to review and select developmentally appropriate software.	3 – 2 – 1
Value 3 – 2 – 1 Demonstrate 3 – 2 – 1	Provide software for the children to work with that mirror skills being worked on in other interest areas.	3 – 2 – 1
Value 3 – 2 – 1 Demonstrate 3 – 2 – 1	Add new software to relate to concepts being introduced, interests expressed by children, field trips taken, etc.	3 – 2 – 1

Key:

Value
3 = highest
1 = lowest

Demonstrate
3 = always
2 = sometimes
1 = rarely

Observation by Supervisor
3 = always
2 = sometimes
1 = rarely

Creative Curriculum Self-Assessment and Observation Form

Teacher: _____

Date of Self-Assessment: _____

Supervisor: _____

Date(s) of Observation: _____

Teacher's Self Assessment	Job Expectations	Supervisor's Observations and Comments
OUTDOORS		
Value 3 --- 2 --- 1 Demonstrate 3 --- 2 --- 1	Arrange the play area so that the view of children is unobstructed and the children understand where the play area begins and ends.	3 --- 2 --- 1
Value 3 --- 2 --- 1 Demonstrate 3 --- 2 --- 1	Include space that fosters both individualized and group play, active and quiet play.	3 --- 2 --- 1
Value 3 --- 2 --- 1 Demonstrate 3 --- 2 --- 1	Select an appropriate public area if there is no outdoor play area adjacent to the classroom.	3 --- 2 --- 1
Value 3 --- 2 --- 1 Demonstrate 3 --- 2 --- 1	Make changes in the daily schedule to accommodate changes in the weather.	3 --- 2 --- 1
Value 3 --- 2 --- 1 Demonstrate 3 --- 2 --- 1	Divide the outdoor area into interest areas such as wheel toys, climbing, woodworking, and water and sand play.	3 --- 2 --- 1
Value 3 --- 2 --- 1 Demonstrate 3 --- 2 --- 1	Plan and discuss scheduling, transportation, materials, equipment with other staff so that children's safety and optimum use of the outdoor space can be ensured.	3 --- 2 --- 1

Key:

Value
3 = highest
1 = lowest

Demonstrate
3 = always
2 = sometimes
1 = rarely

Observation by Supervisor
3 = always
2 = sometimes
1 = rarely

Creative Curriculum Self-Assessment and Observation Form

Teacher: _____

Date of Self-Assessment: _____

Supervisor: _____

Date(s) of Observation: _____

Teacher's Self Assessment	Job Expectations	Supervisor's Observations and Comments
OUTDOORS (Cont'd)		
Value 3 — 2 — 1 Demonstrate 3 — 2 — 1	Design and plan for outdoor activities that meet the children's needs and reflect their interests (e.g., field trips, dramatic play, science experiences, mud play).	3 — 2 — 1
INVOLVING PARENTS IN THE PROGRAM		
Value 3 — 2 — 1 Demonstrate 3 — 2 — 1	Treat each parent with respect.	3 — 2 — 1
Value 3 — 2 — 1 Demonstrate 3 — 2 — 1	Find ways for parents to be involved in the daily program in a meaningful way.	3 — 2 — 1
Value 3 — 2 — 1 Demonstrate 3 — 2 — 1	Discuss parents' expectations and help them understand and appreciate the opportunities for learning in a developmentally appropriate curriculum.	3 — 2 — 1
Value 3 — 2 — 1 Demonstrate 3 — 2 — 1	Provide opportunities for parents to learn about the curriculum and how they extend learning at home.	3 — 2 — 1
Value 3 — 2 — 1 Demonstrate 3 — 2 — 1	Talk with parents regularly about their child's progress.	3 — 2 — 1

Key:

Value
3 = highest
1 = lowest

Demonstrate
3 = always
2 = sometimes
1 = rarely

Observation by Supervisor
3 = always
2 = sometimes
1 = rarely

Appendix B

Staff Development Forms

OBSERVATION OF THE ENVIRONMENT

Teacher:_____

Observer: _____   Date: _____

GENERAL LAYOUT

Room Divided	Variety of materials and textures
Place for each child's belongings	Shelves labeled
Artwork displayed	Diversity reflected in materials

ORGANIZATION OF IDEAS

Blocks	Art
House Corner	Table Toys
Library	Sand and Water
Music and Movement	Cooking
Computers	Outdoors

TEACHER OBSERVATION*	
Teacher: _____	Focus: _____
Observer: _____	Date: _____

Goal	
Setting	

TEACHER	OUTCOME
TEACHER	OUTCOME
TEACHER	OUTCOME
TEACHER	OUTCOME
TEACHER	OUTCOME
TEACHER	OUTCOME
COMMENTS	

*Based on the Council for Early Childhood Professional Recognition, *CDA Representative's Procedures Manual*, Washington, DC: CECPR, 1985.

OBSERVATION SUMMARY

Teacher: _____   Supervisor/Trainer: _____

Date of observation: _____   Focus of observation:_____

(This form is to be completed prior to the conference. Both supervisor/trainer and teacher should have a copy.)

Strengths Observed:

Recommendations:

STAFF DEVELOPMENT WORKSHEET

Teacher:_____   Supervisor:_____

Date: _____

Job behavior: _____

Teacher's goal:

What the teacher will do and by when:

What the supervisor will do and by when:

Date of next observation: